C·A·N·A·D·A

A SYMPHONY IN COLOR

**Text by
Grace Deutsch and Avanthia Swan**

Collins Toronto

BRITISH COLUMBIA

British Columbia is Canada's own Garden of Eden. All of the splendors of creation are to be found in this vast land that covers more than 350,000 square miles. Here, in Canada's most western province, mighty mountains, snow-capped and brooding, stand guard over paradise. Rivers, both furious and fanciful, roll through immense gorges and lush fertile valleys. British Columbia is racing cloud and teeming rain saturating the long winding coast, and bright sun mocking the thirsty plains of the interior. This is a land of contrasts: somber northern woods stretching for thousands of acres, and sensual, moss-hung rain forests dripping with voluptuous lushness; lazy, indolent beaches and tempestuous Pacific breakers; smothering snowstorms and extravagant sunsets; but it is the rainbows with their delicately tinted arches that best symbolize the peace and plentitude of this bountiful province.

So overwhelming is nature's presence in B.C., that it seems almost to have dwarfed the two-and-one-half million people who call the province home. This does not bother British Columbians, but tourists often find beautiful British Columbia somewhat overwhelming. Many first-time visitors to the province have experienced the heady sensation of finding themselves in Vancouver, map in hand, simply unable to decide what to do next. Should they head north to the Cariboo and gold rush country or east to the orchards and vineyards of the Okanagan? Tackle the wild white waters of the Fraser River or the steep mountain trails of lofty Mount Robson, at 12,972 feet the highest peak in the Canadian Rockies? Or perhaps explore cougar country in the ranching region of the interior?

If you take the advice of most British Columbians, you will forget the mainland for a moment. The best orientation to B.C. is time spent on Vancouver Island, that miniature of the mainland just a ferry ride away from the city of Vancouver across the Strait of Georgia. The 300 mile length of Vancouver Island has something of everything that makes the province famous: mountains, valleys, rolling hills, rivers and lakes.

It was the Spanish explorer Juan de Fuca who first sailed the waters of the Pacific in the vicinity of Vancouver Island in 1592. De Fuca mistook the strait that now bears his name for the mythical Strait of Ainam, a marvellous inland sea believed to link the Atlantic to the Pacific.

Delusions concerning this northwest passage continued, inspiring both Britain's Sir Francis Drake, and the Danish explorer, Vitus Bering, in the employ of the Russians, to embark on further explorations in the region.

On March 29, 1778, Captain James Cook landed the *Resolution* and the *Discovery* at Nootka Sound, about

Vancouver these pages *originated in the 1870s as a sawmilling settlement called Granville. It was renamed Vancouver after Captain George Vancouver of the Royal Navy who had navigated the coast in 1792. The residential area alongside Kitsilano Beach is pictured* left, *while above is a view of the Grouse Mountain Sky Ride. An ocean liner leaves the port* top, *and two superb views of the city can be seen* opposite page top and bottom.
Overleaf *A magnificent photograph of Vancouver's magical night-time skyline.*

BRITISH COLUMBIA

Vancouver, illustrated on these pages, is a densely populated city, located on the southwestern edge of British Columbia. It is set in a beautiful landscape which incorporates the wild mountain country of the Coast Range to the north, gentle rolling farmlands and, of course, the Burrard Inlet, a natural harbor around which the city is built. Vancouver is Canada's third largest city, and the pulsating business heart of British Columbia. From Vanier Park can be seen the new high-rise buildings of Vancouver's West End facing page below, and set in the park is the H R MacMillan Planetarium facing page top.

Overleaf The Lions Gate Bridge, just under one mile long, was opened in 1938. Here it is pictured silhouetted against an evening sky, as the city's lights begin to twinkle in the twilight.

midway along the west coast of Vancouver Island, where he was welcomed by the Nootka Indians. The fine sea otter pelts the British acquired through trade with the Nootka fetched a handsome price at the court of the Emperor of China. The British were quick to take advantage of Cook's amicable relationship with the Nootka, to exploit the China trade.

Spanish indignation at this British intrusion into what they considered their North American private preserve knew no bounds. War between Spain and England was only circumvented by the Spanish accession to the old principle that possession is nine-tenths of the law; after all, the British had *occupied* part of Vancouver Island, while the Spanish, unsure of their reception by the

Nootka, had merely sailed along its coast.

It fell to Captain George Vancouver, who had been a young officer on Cook's voyage, to actually sail into Georgia Strait and confirm Vancouver Island's British status, while also exploring the west coast of mainland British Columbia.

The nineteenth century saw Britain's tenuous hold on the island challenged by the restless Americans to the south. Lewis and Clark's famous expedition of 1803 brought the explorers all the way from the Mississippi River to the mouth of the Columbia, causing John Jacob Astor, New York entrepreneur extraordinaire, to see visions of fur forts stretching through the Rockies to the Pacific.

BRITISH COLUMBIA

The Lions Gate Bridge left was built to provide access to the new development of West and North Vancouver across the Burrard Inlet. Two very different views of downtown Vancouver can be seen right and bottom: one is a view from New Courthouse overlooking Robson Square; the other is at night, across False Creek. Leading to downtown Vancouver and Robson Street is busy Cambie opposite page below right, seen here in rush hour. In the 1950s, Germans and other European immigrants opened continental shops and cafés on Robson Street – and it became known as Robson Strasse. An extraordinary view of the Planetarium is shown opposite page below left.

Astor's plans for the northwest did not appeal to the two great fur trading enterprises of British North America, the Hudson's Bay Company and the North West Company. With the Hudson's Bay Company accorded exclusive trading rights east from the Continental Divide to the Great Lakes, the independent Nor'Westers looked upon all the lands west from the Rocky Mountains to the Pacific Coast – which they called New Caledonia – as their preserve.

As a result of the dynamic, if sometimes destructive, competition between the men of the Hudson's Bay Company and the Nor'Westers, by the early years of the nineteenth century all the great Canadian rivers east and west of the Continental Divide had been traversed to their sources and forts had been established all the way to the west coast. In 1821 the rivals merged and spent the next twenty years attempting to hold the Americans at bay, whilst also fending off Russian advances from the north.

With the signing of the Oregon Treaty between Britain and the United States in 1846, the present international border was established at the 49th parallel. When, in 1849, Britain made Vancouver Island a Crown Colony the Hudson's Bay trading post of Fort Victoria was retained as the main center and the island was administered by James Douglas, the senior officer of the Hudson's Bay Company.

Before twenty years had passed, the sleepy little post of not quite five hundred people had burgeoned into a bustling raw frontier town of over 6,000, whose fortunes were made as Fort Victoria served as the commissary for a raggle-taggle collection of over 25,000 men who surged through the town en route to the mainland and the Cariboo gold fields on the Thompson River.

To try to stave off the lawlessness that had characterized the California gold rush of 1849, Governor Douglas compelled all miners to take out a licence in Victoria before they headed over the strait and up the Thompson. At the same time, the Colonial Office in faraway London, fearful lest the United States take advantage of these frenetic times to annex the region, firmly clasped the mainland to Britain's imperial bosom by declaring it a Crown Colony in 1858. Queen Victoria herself named her newest possession "British Columbia," and appointed James Douglas governor of the new colony.

As communities on the mainland grew, the arrival of English farmers and artisans and their families on the island brought a sense of respectable stability to booming Fort Victoria. When the mainland and the island were united into one colony in 1886, the old Hudson's Bay fort came of age as the capital.

As befitted a capital city, Victoria looked to her British roots to find that air of gracious circumspection so appropriate for a seat of government. And today, even though Victoria is resolutely planted in the twentieth century there is time to spare for the little rituals that make life so delightful. Cricket is played with the same languorous civility found on the pitches at Lords. And at the stately Empress Hotel, afternoon tea is a nineteenth-century delight of fine food and perfectly brewed tea all served in the most delicate bone china. The old vine-covered Empress, with its commanding views of Victoria Harbor, was built by the Canadian Pacific Railway in 1905, and has long been the center of Victoria's social life.

By night, Vancouver takes on a unique sequined, sparkling beauty. A view of Water Street in trendy Gastown above looks toward the Harbour Centre Building; from the Royal Vancouver Yacht Club, across Coal Harbour, can be seen the panorama left; and above left is an aerial view of the Hotel Vancouver in the center of the city.
On the opposite page are illustrated the Old Court House Fountain in Robson Square top left; an exotic modern sculpture in front of Eaton's Pacific Centre top right; the glamorous foyer of the Orpheum Theatre bottom left; and the Orpheum's elegant auditorium bottom right, where the Vancouver Symphony Orchestra can be seen playing.

BRITISH COLUMBIA

Architectural reminders of the old queen's reign dot the city. Dr. Sebastian Helmcken's house on Belleville Street still stands much as it did when the young doctor set up housekeeping with his bride, Cecilia (one of Governor Douglas's daughters) in 1852. The doctor, who first came to Canada as a ship's physician on a Hudson's Bay trading vessel, went on to take his place in the province's first legislative assembly, and skilfully negotiated B.C.'s entry into Canadian Confederation in 1871.

Almost neighbors with the Helmckens was the family of Peter O'Reilly, whose fine old home, Point Ellice House, gazes out over the north shore of the island's Inner Harbor. As Stipendary Magistrate and Assistant Gold Commissioner, O'Reilly was responsible for maintaining law and order among the rowdy miners of the mainland gold rush towns.

And then there are the Parliament Buildings, opened in February 1898 – splendidly structured with inlaid mosaic-tiled floors, stained glass windows, marble panels, and an abundance of that busy gilded plaster work so beloved by Victorian architects and builders.

Victoria's buildings, both old and new, are enhanced by a series of magnificent parks that lie like verdant oases among the bricks and mortar of the city. Blessed with mild winters and balmy summers, Victoria is a gardener's delight. From Crystal Garden's exotic blooms and Beacon Hill Park's intricately designed flower gardens and quiet ponds to the fragrant rose bushes surrounding almost every home, Victoria's love affair with trees, shrubs and flowers has made the city the envy of the rest of Cana-

dians, locked as they are in more chilly climes.

Picnicking on Beacon Hill, with the sunlight dancing on the waters of nearby Juan de Fuca Strait, and the Olympic Mountains looming across the waters in Washington State, the visitor is disinclined to ever leave Victoria. In fact, many Canadians, having once come to the city, determine to spend their retirement years here.

North of Victoria is the Saanich Peninsula. Here, above the gentle farmlands and quiet coastal beaches, the pure song of the skylark, introduced to the island by homesick English settlers, can be heard. No visit in the

Horseshoe Bay above left serves as a ferry port for travelers to Vancouver Island. Point Atkinson Lighthouse above is seen here against a perfect blue sky; and the coastal scenery around Vancouver top has all the romance and variety to captivate even the most seasoned traveler. Kitsilano Beach and swimming pool right – a summer playground for residents and tourists alike. Brightly decked-out boats are reflected in the waters of the Royal Vancouver Yacht Club top right, set in Stanley Park. This park was dedicated in 1889, "to the use and enjoyment of people of all colors, creeds and customs, for all time."

BRITISH COLUMBIA

Saanich is complete without seeing the Butchart Gardens on Brentwood Bay. A paradise reclaimed from the maw of an old quarry, the vast amphitheater is a mass of shrubs and trees and elegantly styled gardens.

Sheltered from the Pacific by Vancouver Island, the Gulf Islands enjoy the mildest winter climate in Canada and are the year-round home of many of Canada's artists, writers, potters and weavers. Saltspring, Mayne, North and South Pender, Galiano, Saturna, Thetis and a hundred or so smaller islands – their beaches seem inexhaustibly stocked with clams and oysters and crabs, and their waters with fish. Deer roam the islands, occasionally sampling the produce in the backyard gardens. It is hard to imagine a better life than that enjoyed by Gulf Islanders – close enough to town should a little urban diversion be needed, yet secluded and safe from the grinding daily pace of big city living.

Further up Vancouver Island's coast is Port Alberni, site of the enormous MacMillan Bloedel pulp and paper mill. The biggest trees in the world grow in the marvellous rain forests of the Pacific coast, and nowhere are the

In British Columbia downhill skiing is an extremely popular sport, and the province's largest ski area is at Whistler Mountain. Whistler Ski Village facing page below is a new and very luxurious ski resort. The photographs these pages were taken at the Molson World Downhill 1982. The fireworks display far right is a spectacular event which takes place the night before the race. On the day, all the competitors ski down the run carrying the flags of their own nations facing page top. The winner, Peter Mueller of Switzerland, and the runner-up, Canadian Steve Podborski, can be seen right waving at the crowd while above right people flock to watch the prize-giving ceremony.

stands more spectacular than the huge Douglas firs found in MacMillan Provincial Park. Here, in aptly named Cathedral Grove, firs more than 600 years old tower 225 feet or more up into the heavens.

Nowhere on Vancouver Island are you far from the Pacific, an ocean of many moods. At one moment, she can be romantic and tender, her gentle waves lapping at the feet of lovers strolling along her solitary shores, the dying evening sun lending a golden glow to the rippling water. The following day, while sunbathers loll on the beach, lazily watched by sea lions taking their leisure on nearby rocks, the ocean can be skittish and playful, delighting surfers and fishermen with her booming waves. And then, as if weary of humanity, she can whip herself into a frenzy of crashing, seething breakers that slam into the coast, goaded on by sullen storm-scoured skies, clamoring thunder, and streaming rain.

But if you can, visit the Pacific at Long Beach, that

marvellous crescent of yellow sand and tidal flats in the Pacific Rim National Park, as the morning mists recede. Fresh driftwood and, perhaps, the odd little glass fishing float, trinket from a fisherman's net in far away Japan, tell of the visitation of the night tides. With the wind-hardened Sitka spruce at your back, and the endless blue of the Pacific seeming to merge with the sky somewhere in another world before you, it is impossible not to feel part of the very act of creation itself.

From the west coast of Vancouver Island you may continue through the rugged wilderness of the interior to Strathcona Provincial Park, where the last of Vancouver Island's elk feed along with wolverine, cougar, coast deer and wolves, and on up to the rich farmland and chinook salmon-packed Campbell River area of the northeast coast, until you reach Kelsey Bay. From here the *Queen of Prince Rupert* departs for its slow trek up the rugged, austere western coast of the B.C. mainland to Prince

Rupert, the province's most northerly anchor.

From Prince Rupert, the Queen Charlotte Islands, about 150 miles north of Vancouver Island, may be reached by plane, freighter, or car ferry. The Queen Charlottes, made up of the two main islands, Graham and Moresby, and many smaller islands, are not for everyone. The silent forests and stern mountains do not offer the easy affability of their southern sisters in the warm ocean stream of the gulf, although winters are relatively mild, thanks to the Great Kuroshio (Japan) Current. Roads are rough, electricity scarce, and lumber camps, iron mines, and crab canneries, while providing work, do not always make for pretty pictures for the family album. Yet there is a primeval beauty in the wildness of these islands that speaks forcefully to artist and adventurer alike. No one

appreciated their magic better than Emily Carr (1871-1945), one of Canada's foremost painters.

Although brought up in genteel Victoria, Emily Carr made periodic trips to the Charlottes. Her bold canvases capture the untamed splendor of the whole west coast, and provide a record of the past glory of the Haida people for whom the islands have been home since the beginning of time.

To return from the Queen Charlottes to Prince Rupert on the mainland is a jolt. Built around a magnificent natural ice-free harbor, Prince Rupert has long been known as the halibut capital of the world. Her large fishing fleet also hauls in fine catches of herring, salmon, lingcod, and sole. Prince Rupert, the second most important B.C. port after Vancouver, is the western terminus of the Canadian

Pacific Rim National Park these pages *is situated on the west coast of Vancouver Island. It stretches from Port Renfrew to Tofino, and one of its most outstanding features is Long Beach* this page and opposite page below. *The park is divided into three main sections: Long Beach, a section which not only covers* the coastline but also the rain forests opposite page top left and right; *Barkley Sound, including the Broken Islands Group; and the West Coast Trail, a wilderness between Bamfield and Port Renfrew. The trail itself was established for shipwrecked sailors who could walk inland and find this pathway to civilization.*

National Railway, which brings the golden harvests of the prairies' wheat here to be shipped abroad.

From Prince Rupert the Yellowhead Highway goes east, following first the Skeena and then the Bulkley River through high canyons and rocky mountains to Prince George, the commercial center of northcentral British Columbia.

The communities in the vast region between the two Princes are as varied as the landscape itself. Aluminium built Kitimat, south of the Skeena, on the Kitimat River. Here aluminium from Australia and Jamaica is processed at the enormous Alcan smelter. Over three million tons of aluminium ingots are shipped annually from Kitimat. Salmon, fighting their way up the narrow gorge of the Bulkley River to spawn, make nearby Moricetown a favorite spot for those daring enough to mount the rocks lining the gorge in order to spear a leaping fish. Ranches and farms, watered by countless rivers, surround Vanderhoof, the geographical center of British Columbia.

From Prince George the Hart Highway leads

BRITISH COLUMBIA

northeast to Dawson Creek, the southern terminus of the Alaska Highway and the "capital" of B.C.'s Peace River Region. Alexander Mackenzie crossed the area in 1793 while in pursuit of an overland route to the Pacific. And Simon Fraser established trading posts for the North West Company along the Peace, Athabaska and Liard rivers, the major waterways of the region. Today, five highways, two railways, an airport, and a sea-plane base confirm Dawson Creek's importance as a lifeline to the north.

Besides its coal and petroleum reserves and the vast hydro electric power capacity generated by the Peace River powerhouse, formed by the construction of the W. A. C. Bennett Dam near the town of Hudson Hope, the Peace River region is also rich agricultural territory, an extension of the neighboring prairies to the east.

But if the Peace, Athabaska, and Liard Rivers mean life to B.C.'s north, the whole province actually came into being around the fierce, fast-flowing Fraser River. Rising at 52°45′ north latitude, the Fraser begins its life innocuously enough in two small streams fed by the glacier of towering Mount Robson, the highest peak in the Rocky Mountains.

The Fraser River is about 850 miles long, and for most of this distance it is a bucking, savage river, constantly fighting the maze of mountains and ridges which, save for the last eighty miles of its course, everywhere attempt to subvert its efforts to flow to the Pacific. In its careening path across the province's interior, the Fraser stains itself a seething muddy yellow from the silt it has robbed from the mountains en route.

The swift waters of the Fraser once forced the Cariboo Mountains to yield another yellowy substance –

BRITISH COLUMBIA

gold. To the depression-wracked world of the late 1850s, rumors of the vast riches to be had in Cariboo country were all that was needed to start a stampede up the Fraser in pursuit of fine placer gold and the heavier solid nuggets lying in the gravel, sand and bedrock of the Fraser and Thompson rivers, their tributaries and streams.

Americans, French, Germans, Chinese, Italians – all were driven by gold fever to risk their lives ascending the Fraser to pan the sand-bars at Hope and Yale, Williams Lake and Quesnel, Barkerville and Soda Creek. Many never made it, and perished in the swirling waters of the Fraser, leaving their foolish wooden rafts to bounce drunkenly along on the river as a testimony to the folly of human dreams.

Apart from providing the nucleus of the mainland's population, the Cariboo gold rush had another vital by-product for B.C.'s development – the Cariboo Road.

It was Governor James Douglas who first realized that something had to be done for the gold-hungry miners who, lemming-like, rushed to their doom in the stern Cariboo canyons, ill-supplied for the rigors of a mountain winter. Douglas had the Royal Engineers build a route into the interior that was, and still is, one of the most awesome and risky roads in North America. When finished, the Cariboo Road, some eighteen feet in width, hugged the canyon cliffs of the Fraser for 385 torturous miles. Mule trains traversed the route bringing supplies to the mining camps further north. With drops of thousands of feet from

The absolutely magnificent gardens illustrated on these pages were once a quarry for Robert Pim Butchart's cement plant! In 1904 Mr. and Mrs. Butchart decided to transform the bleak quarry, and began by planting a few roses and sweet peas. From this small beginning grew a dedicated and expensive hobby, as the Butcharts began to collect flowers and plants from all over the world. The Sunken Garden was transformed into a great bowlful of color, which overflowed into the Rose Garden, the Italian Garden and the Japanese Garden. They named their gardens "Benvenuto," the Italian word for "Welcome," and everyone is welcome to come and enjoy the wonderful Butchart Gardens. Over half a million photographs are taken here annually, and the gardens feature blooms of every season.
Overleaf Cottonwood House near Quesnel.

the road's unguarded lip, horse, mule or man need only stumble once to plunge to a sorry end below.

No one would have applauded the road more than Simon Fraser, for whom the river is named. In 1808, fifty years before the first miners struggled north into Cariboo country, Fraser had led a small expedition down the raging river he erroneously believed to be the Columbia. Starting at Prince George, the party travelled downriver in birchbark canoes into the seething melee of the canyon that, likewise, bears his name. Here, amidst towering cliffs, they were carried along at frightful speeds by the remorseless pull of the Fraser's currents, and spun dizzyingly through her whirlpools until finally they were swept ashore.

Of Hell's Gate, the Canyon's narrows, the dour Fraser recorded in his journal: "I have ... never seen anything like this country. It is so wild I cannot find words to describe it at times. We had to pass where no human being should venture ...".

The Fraser's tributaries, the Thompson and the Chilcotin, water the vast "Dry Belt" of the British Columbia interior, where herds of cattle graze the open ranges. In contrast to cattle country is the broad valley of the Fraser itself, once it has broken out of its mountain fastness at Hope, an old trading post of the Hudson's Bay Company. Its destiny at last assured, the turbulent river

Since 1958, when the Barkerville Restoration Committee began its work, this gold town has been lovingly resurrected. Right and top left *St. Saviours Anglican Church at the end of the main street;* left *the printing office of the "Cariboo Sentinel";* below right *the Barkerville Hotel; and* below left *Main Street.* Opposite page *The annual Prince George Professional Rodeo.* Overleaf *Evening draws in over Lillooet Lake.*

BRITISH COLUMBIA

flows serenely through the fertile farms and well-tended acres of heavily populated southwestern B.C. Its massive silt deposits make the lower Fraser Valley one of the richest agricultural regions in Canada, able to feed not only booming B.C., but also to provide a surplus for her export markets.

Fittingly, at the mouth of this historic river is Vancouver, Canada's third largest city and her window on the Pacific.

Vancouver is an architect's delight. Here, where the Pacific meets the coast in a series of marvellous beaches and the Fraser flows languorously to meet the ocean, protected by the watchful Coast Mountains, the architectural efforts of man are displayed to best effect.

With a population of over one-and-one-quarter million, and growing fast, Metropolitan Vancouver stretches in all directions, taking in the communities of North Vancouver, Port Coquitlam, Port Moody, Richmond, Burnaby, Surrey, White Rock, Delta, Lions Bay, Pitt Meadows, Langley City, Langley, and New Westminster. Ironically, no one expected that Vancouver would one day be B.C.'s premier city. Victoria and New Westminster were the chief rivals for the honor.

New Westminster was the capital of British Columbia from 1859 to 1868 but when Vancouver Island and the mainland were united in 1866, Victoria was chosen, after some dispute, as the capital.

The following year saw the confederation of the four eastern Crown Colonies (Ontario, Quebec, New Brunswick, Nova Scotia) into the Dominion of Canada.

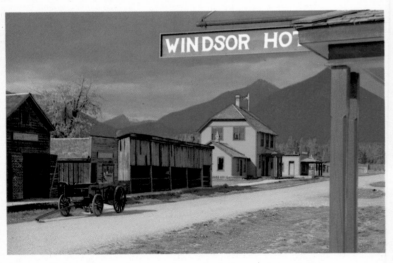

Situated in the Fort Steele Historic Park is a reconstructed Kootenay town of the 1890-1905 period. Fort Steele above, right, top right and opposite page top, overlooking the Kootenay River, was a ghost town after World War II, then came back to life in the 1960s. Center right The CN Railway crossing the North Thompson River; opposite page below Three Valley Gap frontier town near Revelstoke. Overleaf A sawmill on the shore of Lake Slocan near Nelson.

B.C.'s newly arrived governor, Anthony Musgrave, worried over the uneasy relations between British Columbia and the United States, championed the idea of B.C.'s joining the new Dominion, even though 3,000 miles lay between Canada and the west coast.

When the promise of a transcontinental railway lured

BRITISH COLUMBIA

B.C. into Confederation, the chosen terminus of the Canadian Pacific Railway was, to the surprise of everyone, the harbor on Burrard Inlet adjacent to Gastown, or Granville, as it was officially known. Gastown had grown around a lumber camp and saw mill and had been named, derisively, after a pub, "Gassy Jack's".

To mark this auspicious event, Gastown's name was changed yet again, this time to Vancouver, in honor of Captain George Vancouver who had dropped anchor in Burrard Inlet in 1792. Shortly before Queen Victoria's birthday celebrations in 1887, the first passenger train arrived in Vancouver. Already her harbor was filled with the tall sails of the Canadian Pacific Railway's China tea clippers, and when the Cunard Line's *Abyssinia* arrived from the Orient with its cargo of transPacific mail and Chinese silk, Vancouver's destiny as Canada's most important Pacific city was assured.

Some of the country's most strikingly innovative

Here in British Columbia, vast regions of virtual wilderness are to be found, all cared for by British Columbians themselves – people who take a protective pride in their environment. The B.C. Forest Service, alongside other conservationists, has worked hard to reclothe the landscape in its natural woodland cover, much of which was indiscriminately cleared by the forest industry. Over 100 million seedlings are planted annually, and harvesting is, in general, restricted to government-designated areas. As each area is cleared, so it is replanted. The lakeside scenery is, perhaps, the loveliest: opposite page bottom right *is Pavillion Lake near Lillooet, and* right *is Burns Lake. The blossoming orchards* opposite page top *enhance the Okanagan Valley every spring.*

modern buildings have been erected here. Taking their tone from Vancouver's splendid natural setting and its equitable climate, buildings like Simon Fraser University on Burnaby Mountain, the work of architect Arthur Erickson, and the futuristic MacMillan Planetarium, are indicative of a very distinct west coast style of architecture. As Vancouverites seem happiest when outdoors, their homes feature expansive airy windows that not only let in lots of natural light, but also permit constant views of nature's changing faces.

Vancouverites love the outdoors. Much to the chagrin of their fellow Canadians, they are known to skip an afternoon's work for a leisurely sail on beautiful English Bay, or a cooling dip in the blue Pacific at Kitsilano Beach. In winter, with Grouse Mountain just twenty minutes away and its snow-covered top well illuminated, after-work skiing becomes a part of daily life.

While the coastal mountains are a hiker's paradise,

BRITISH COLUMBIA

more sedate walkers may take their leisure in any of Vancouver's 144 parks, of which the largest is Stanley Park. Situated on a peninsula jutting out into Burrard Inlet, Stanley Park covers some 1,000 acres, and was originally a military encampment in the days when an American attack was considered imminent. In 1889 Governor-General Lord Stanley declared the area to be a park intended for "the use and enjoyment of peoples of all colors, creeds and customs". Although guns were installed to protect Burrard Inlet and English Bay from possible enemy attack during World Wars I and II, the park is today a haven of peace and serenity. The park's zoo is home to a splendid collection of king penguins, not to mention polar bears, otters and seals.

Both the Vandusen Botanical Display Garden and Queen Elizabeth Park on top of Little Mountain are well worth a visit. The Nitobe Memorial Gardens on the north-western edge of the University of British Columbia is considered by some Vancouverites to be the city's love-liest park. An authentic Japanese garden complete with bonsai and a teahouse and snow temple, the Nitobe Gardens convey the delicate purity of a pearl offset by the exuberant brilliance of a surround of emeralds and rubies.

But what of Vancouverites themselves? Unlike some eastern cities to which migration from other than English-speaking lands (or French-speaking, in the case of Quebec communities) is a fairly recent phenomenon, Vancouver, and British Columbia, have long been home to many non-British groups. In fact, it could well be argued that British Columbia was actually built by the industry of the Chinese.

In Mount Robson Provincial Park above the mountain looms behind Robson River; blue skies are reflected in Slocan Lake above left; sunlight dapples the hillsides around Kamloops Lake right; and the Skeena River runs between pine-clad shores above right.
Overleaf A dramatic view of the Fraser River near Lillooet.

Hardworking, and motivated by the desire to help their families back home, 15,000 Chinese men came to Canada to labor on the backbreaking, dangerous work of building the transcontinental railway. They worked in the coal mines around Nanaimo on Vancouver Island, and maintained the homes and gardens of Victoria's new millionaires. On the mainland they panned for gold, and were sent deep into the interior to fell the lumber on which B.C.'s economic well-being depended. Shamefully exploited and, on occasion, subjected to violent racial abuse, B.C.'s Chinese nevertheless persevered. Today, they work in all professions. Vancouver's Chinatown, the largest in North America after San Francisco, abounds in fine restaurants and shops filled with exotic merchandise from the Orient. All of Vancouver joins in the celebration of Chinese New Year, a riotous extravaganza of dragons and drums, parades and firecrackers, and loads of good things to eat.

B.C.'s once large Japanese community, uprooted during the frightened days of World War II, has never quite returned to its former strength. But its contribution to B.C. cultural life far outstrips its limited numbers.

Most of the nations of Europe are represented in Vancouver, as also are immigrants from the East Indies. It is this diversity that is responsible for the vitality and verve

BRITISH COLUMBIA

that characterizes this city that grew up around old Gassy Jack's pub.

Today Gastown lives again in a restoration of the old waterfront community. Smart restaurants, bars and fashionable boutiques now fill the once dilapidated warehouses and "two-bit" hotels of the old town.

Less than 250 miles from Vancouver, the sunny Okanagan Valley is a land of orchards and vineyards, bountiful lakes and peaceful, prosperous towns like Penticton, Peachland, Vernon and Kelowna, which nestle safely in the shelter of distant mountains. Apples, apricots, peaches, pears, plums, nectarines, melons, cherries, and grapes grow in the Okanagan, thanks to irrigation which has turned the valley's once dry slopes into a fertile orchard.

Apple growing was first introduced into the Okanagan by Father Charles Pandosy in 1859. From that modest beginning at Kelowna, the area now supplies one-third of all Canada's apples.

The northern end of the valley is dairy country, and world-renowned for its excellent cheese.

With fresh produce available from most Okanagan farms, and the sun-ripened bounty of her vineyards readily to hand, a chunk of Okanagan cheddar and some homemade bread complete the perfect picnic lunch. And there is no shortage of secluded country roads whose shady nooks by quiet streams seem just made for a well-stocked hamper and a long, indolent afternoon.

Next door to the Okanagan Valley is the Kootenay region. Silver put the Kootenays on the map, and the skeleton reminders of once booming silver towns live on among the ever encroaching forests.

Most eastern Canadians return home with at least one full roll of film devoted to the Kootenays. It is a beautiful region, full of rolling green valleys, snow-mantled mountains, cool forests, and rivers and lakes brimming with rainbow and Dolly Varden trout and kokanee salmon.

In southcentral British Columbia, visitors can only marvel at the sight of the Adams River turning crimson as two million sockeye salmon make their way here up the Thompson and Fraser rivers to spawn and, their four-year lifecycle complete, to waste away and die.

Sadly, only expert skiers can enjoy the thrill of exploring the prehistoric world of Asulkan Valley in Glacier National Park, part of the ancient Selkirk Mountains, that wild range formed millions of years before the Rocky Mountains came into being. There are more than one hundred glaciers in this park, creating a landscape more terrestrial than earthlike.

East from Glacier National Park the Trans Canada Highway follows the Illecillewaet, Columbia and Kicking Horse rivers through mountain fortresses and meadows of brilliant wildflowers over Kicking Horse Pass and into Yoho National Park in the Rockies. Here, visitors may marvel at Takakkaw Falls, a twelve-hundred-foot cascade of spume-tossed splendor. The Indians called this ever-changing wilderness "yoho," an expression of their wonder and astonishment at its beauty. As anyone who knows British Columbia will attest, it is a term for the whole province, for the range and generosity of nature's gifts to B.C. are truly awe inspiring.

Above *Westbank, Okanagan Lake*; center *Prince George from Connaught Hill Park*; top *Prince Rupert*; right and above far right *Golden, Kicking Horse River*; above right *Nelson on Kokanee Creek*

GOLDEN

This was once the loading point for Upper Columbia sternwheelers. Completion of the C.P.R. in 1886 heralded the steamboat era when colourful little craft like the "Duchess" freighted to Columbia Lake and waypoints. Smelters built in 1904-05 were never "blown in". Camps, steamers and smelters have gone, but Golden thrives because of its strategic location on the nation's major travel routes.

PROVINCE OF
BRITISH COLUMBIA
19 70

ALBERTA

Ask Canadians what Alberta means to them and they will likely tell you: "oil," "the Rocky Mountains," "cattle," "oil," "wheat," "the Calgary Stampede," "oil," "opportunity," "skiing," "oil," "natural gas," "the Badlands," "oil," "oil," "oil"...

Thanks to her large oil deposits Alberta, Canada's most recently settled province, stands poised to overtake Ontario and become the nation's economic leader. While the population of Canada increased by only five percent during the last five years, Alberta's population has grown by over twenty percent in the same period, due largely to the prosperity generated by oil.

Calgary, the province's "oil capital," has grown faster than any other city in Canada. Over the last half-decade, people from all across Canada and around the world have flocked to participate in Alberta's boom.

It is a pulsating, zesty city, this northern Dallas, considered brash and pushy by the long established power centers of eastern Canada. But for those with the energy and the spirit to accept a challenge, Calgary is the very heart of the new frontier.

The Alaska Highway these pages runs from Fairbanks in the State of Alaska to "Mile-O" at Dawson Creek in B.C. The drive has been called the experience of a lifetime, and it is easy to see why. Much of the road is narrow, winding, and very dusty – and the dust manages to find its way everywhere! Despite broad daylight, it is necessary to drive with headlights on to see through the dust.... Both headlights and windscreens get broken, and the driver is frequently subjected to "freeze-ups" or "washouts." This may sound like a nightmare, but the Alaska Highway is, almost always, referred to with affection by the drivers who tackle it regularly.

ALBERTA

The capital of Alberta is Edmonton *these pages*, a city with a population of over half a million. *Downtown Edmonton* left *has a seemingly ever-changing sky-line as new buildings grow skywards. The Provincial Museum* opposite page below *was completed in 1967 to coincide with, and commemorate, Canada's Centennial Year. The history of Alberta is laid out in the museum, exhibits including displays of early Indian life and pioneer settlement as well as geology and natural history. Ultramodern architecture characterizes parts of Edmonton, as seen beside the Court House* opposite page top, *and at the Muttart Conservatory* below. *This extraordinary structure is a series of pyramids, each containing a different environment and climate.*

Situated about 350 miles north of the Canadian/United States border, Edmonton these pages is the most northerly of Canada's major cities. The Rocky Mountains lie about 200 miles to the west. The climate in Edmonton ranges from very warm summers to winters when the temperature falls well below the freezing point. The fact that it is located so far north means that the city has very few daylight hours in winter – about seven – and very long days in the summer – up to seventeen hours of daylight. The history of Edmonton dates back to 1795, when the first Fort Edmonton was built at the confluence of the North Saskatchewan and Sturgeon rivers. The skyline of the city is seen left behind the North Saskatchewan River from the James Macdonald Bridge; while the more hectic scene of Jasper Avenue in rush hour is shown below. The University of Alberta is pictured opposite page top, and the Muttart Conservatory below left and opposite page below.

Some 500 oil and gas exploration companies have their head office in Calgary. The construction industry is booming here as shimmering skyscrapers race each other to tower majestically over the prairies, flaunting their grandeur before the ever-present skyline of the Rocky Mountains to the west.

Calgary's burgeoning population has caused an acute housing shortage. It is not a shortage of land that is the problem – Calgary's well-planned, spacious suburbs sprawl out onto the surrounding prairies – it is that with so much commercial building going on, and with so many newcomers arriving in Calgary, residential building cannot keep up with the demand.

Much of Alberta's oil development was pioneered by Americans from Texas and Oklahoma. As a result, Calgary is undoubtedly the most American of all Canada's cities.

That spirit of expansiveness and reckless daring which constantly propels Americans forward is alive and thriving on Calgary's Centre Street.

Calgary's present affluence has its origins in the 1912 discovery of oil at nearby Turner Valley, the first significant oilfield discovered in the British Empire. Although Turner Valley continued to produce oil through the twenties and thirties, supplying not quite ten percent of Canada's needs, it was the 1947 discovery of the huge Leduc oilfield, south of Edmonton, that really made the province wealthy. Here at Leduc, amidst the waving grain fields of Alberta's prairies, black gold gushed forth from Imperial's Leduc No.1 well. Before making its momentous strike on February 13, 1947, Imperial Oil had drilled 113 dry holes. But No.1 well opened up a field that was to yield over 300-million barrels of crude oil.

ALBERTA

Albertans scarcely had time to raise their champagne glasses when a massive blow-out at nearby Atlantic No.3 well drove home the dangers inherent in their new-found treasure. In March 1947, Atlantic No.3 went out of control and for the next six months spewed oil all over the prairie. Then it burst into flames. Plugging Atlantic No.3 took 20,000 bags of cement, 16,000 bags of sawdust, 1,000 sacks of cottonwood hulls, 8 railway carloads of wood fiber, and 2 carloads of turkey feathers.

Sobered, but undaunted, Albertans continued their quest for oil. By 1948 there were twenty-three producing wells in the Leduc field and wildcat drilling had uncovered oil at Woodbend, west of Edmonton, and at Redwater, to the north. Today, the province has close to 12,000 oil wells, spread over some thirty major fields.

Edmonton, the provincial capital, was originally a Hudson's Bay Company trading post and the old fort lives on in a faithful reconstruction. But it was gold, not furs, that first boosted Edmonton's fortune. The community became a supply base for those travelling westward through the Rockies to the Klondike Gold Fields in '98. And every July, Edmontonians dress themselves and their handsome modern city in nineteenth century garb and give themselves over to a riotous celebration of the roaring nineties.

Today, gold has given place to oil. Edmonton is right in the middle of that part of Alberta which supplies over eighty percent of Canada's oil. More than 2,000 wells are situated within twenty-five miles of the city.

The walking-horse oil pumps have become a symbol for the province. The pumps seem to be everywhere; the rhythmic squeak of the pumper carrying over the sighing prairie winds as the walking-horse beam rocks to and fro and the sucker rods pull up the oil. Not so long ago, when it seemed that oil and gas would last forever, the gas that was extracted along with the oil was simply burnt off. Now it is piped to waiting markets in industrial eastern Canada.

Some 360,000,000 years ago, during that period geologists call the Upper Devonian, Alberta was covered by the enormous, shallow Mowry Sea. The waters teemed

Calgary these pages lies where the Bow and Elbow rivers meet and the name "Calgary" is Gaelic for "clear running water." The modern skyline is dominated by the Calgary Tower, featured in these photographs. The tower reaches a height of 620 feet, and houses an observation deck and a revolving restaurant.

with plankton, tiny one-celled animals and plants that floated by the billions near the surface of the sea. Scientists believe that oil and gas were formed from the liquid contained in those single celled plankton.

Present technology enables the extraction of about forty-five percent of Alberta's known oil reserves. The rest is still trapped in the earth beyond our reach.

Far greater wealth than that found in Alberta's conventional oil fields lies in the Athabasca Tar Sands in the province's northeast corner. Geologists estimate the tar sands contain at least 900,000,000,000 barrels of oil. Getting at this treasure calls for an entirely different approach; mining, not drilling, will free Athabasca's oil, and the techniques needed will make the extraction an extremely costly operation.

ALBERTA

Alberta's other major geological legacy, the spectacular Rocky Mountains, are readily accessible to all.

The same sea that bequeathed Alberta its oil is also responsible for the Rocky Mountains. The build-up of sediment on the floor of the Mowry Sea had slowly turned to rock, then tumultous convulsions beneath the earth's crust thrust these rock-layers eastward, forcing them to crease and buckle like a giant accordion.

Four great Ice Ages came and went, each time altering the face of this mountain kingdom. Where once the Rocky Mountains were rounded and scored by river valleys, the ice-age glaciers carved the mountains into towering ridges and awesome peaks. The great tongues of ice gouged out deep basins. As the ice melted, it turned these basins into enormous blue-green lakes. Banff's Lake

Calgary is vibrant with life and energy – these being epitomized by the Calgary Stampede these and the following pages, a spectacular event held annually. The city has blossomed and grown over the last hundred years, and although it is in all senses a modern city, here the old west lives on. When the railroad was built it brought merchants and missionaries, ranchers and farmers, remittance men and, inevitably, a few scoundrels! Sarcee, Blood, Blackfoot, Stony and Piegan Indians came to trade here, and great herds of cattle were brought from the overgrazed ranches south of the border, to feed on the lush "short grass" which is so perfectly suited to raising prime beef animals.

ALBERTA

Louise is perhaps the most well-known and one of the loveliest of these lakes.

The Rockies are always changing. Vast permanent icefields in the high mountains of Alberta, the Yukon and British Columbia continue to spawn glaciers. These rivers of ice are nature's chisels, which continue to alter the face of the Rockies. The most famous of the Rocky Mountain icefields is the enormous Columbia Icefield, which straddles the boundary between Banff and Jasper national parks. With an area of 120 square miles and up to 3,000 feet thick in places, the Columbia Icefield nurtures the Athabasca Glacier, itself at least six miles long and up to 2,000 feet thick.

Banff National Park, some ninety miles from Calgary and easily reached by road or air, covers an enormous 2,564 square miles. Under skies of unrivalled brilliance, Banff in summer is a world of endless forests marching to meet snow-veiled mountains. Meadows here are afire with a million alpine blooms and lakes, colored astonishing emerald greens and sapphire blues by tiny particles of suspended glacial debris, mirror the mountains that encircle their loveliness.

Banff is for everyone – hikers, canoeists, fishermen, mountain climbers, horseback riders and nature lovers of all ages.

Winter snows accentuate the immensity of the park. Away from the busy ski slopes and the whoops and hollers of sleighriders and tobogganers, quietly slogging through Banff's deep drifts on snowshoes, the park's pristine beauty is dazzling, its mysterious, silent aloofness disquietening even to the most solitary of individuals.

Nestling trustingly in the shadow of these mountain fasts, is the town of Banff, a permanent community of over 3,000 people. Here on the Bow River, which runs through the town, the elegant Banff Springs Hotel graces the winter scene like a fairy palace out of the brothers Grimm.

Actually a bit of natural magic was responsible for the park's existence. In 1883, workmen building the Canadian Pacific Railway through the Rockies noticed wisps of steam coming from a hole in the ground on the south side of the Bow Valley. Investigation revealed a cavern containing a pool of steaming, sulphurous water.

A Calgary tourist brochure eloquently describes the Calgary Stampede these pages in the following words: "The Greatest Dad-Burned Outdoor Show on Earth, held annually early in July. Ten days of western fun and excitement, ushered in by the spectacular Stampede parade, chuckwagon breakfasts... square dancing in the streets ...parades of Mounties and Indians, cowboys, and pioneers each morning...world championship rodeo... chuckwagon races...dazzling stage shows with star celebrities... gambling casinos...nightclubs with entertainment from mild to wild. Don't just come to watch – come to participate!!"
Yes, for ten days every July,

Calgary lives it up. Flapjacks and coffee, grandstand shows and fireworks, livestock exhibits, a huge funfair, and a village with Stony, Sarcee, Blood and Blackfoot Indians. Cowboys from all over Canada and the United States compete in the rodeo for prize-money amounting to over a quarter of a million dollars! And daily events include saddle and bareback bronco busting, Brahma bull and buffalo riding, a wild-horse race, steer wrestling, calf-roping and wrestling, wild-cow milking and the world-famous Royal Canadian Mounted Police Musical Wagon Ride.

Overleaf Columbia Icefield, Jasper National Park.

ALBERTA

Taking the waters quickly caught on, even though getting to them was not all that easy. One early hotelier used to raft his guests across the Bow River to the springs on railway ties lashed together with telegraph wire! In 1885, the area, then known as Rocky Mountain Park, came under federal government jurisdiction. Today, pools fed by the hot springs await visitors who have spent a hard day on the slopes or in the saddle.

Banff has another famous attraction – the Banff Centre of Fine Arts. Opened as a summer theater school in 1933, Banff attracts the best young Canadian talent in music, theater, and the visual arts. And certainly not since the open-air theaters of the ancient Greeks, have the arts enjoyed a more inspired setting!

Calgarians, while happy to share Banff with everyone, look upon it as their natural playground, considering it the fairest of the Rocky Mountain parks. Their northern neighbors, and friendly rivals, in Edmonton, maintain that Jasper National Park, which adjoins Banff at the Columbia Icefield, outdoes its sister in the grandeur of its mountains, the brilliance of its glaciers, and the bracing crispness of its clear alpine air.

In 1907 the opening of the transcontinental railway link through Yellowhead Pass meant that Jasper's rugged beauty was now accessible to all. Where once trappers, missionaries, geologists, prospectors, and surveyors went about their solitary work, now visitors from all over the world come here to hike some of North America's finest backcountry trails, canoe Jasper's wild rivers, fish its still lakes, relax in its hot springs, tackle the park's giant peaks, and admire the animals that make their home here.

Jasper's 4,200 square miles shelter grizzly and black bears, herds of mule deer, graceful bighorn sheep, nimble

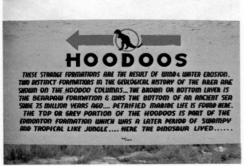

The eerie rock formations above right *can be found in the Valley of the Dinosaurs near Drumheller. The scenery was created millions of years ago by glacial action, and what was once a tropical marshland inhabited by pre-historic reptiles is now a naturalist's paradise. Dinosaur Provincial Park* right *and facing page top is famous for its spectacular badland scenery and its dinosaur quarries and displays. Writing-on-Stone Provincial Park* facing page below *lies in the short-grass prairie region of Alberta, and was named after the Indian rock carvings and paintings which were found on the massive sandstone outcrops. The wind-and-rain sculpted rocks or hoodoos referred to in the notice* above *provide an other-worldly atmosphere.*

A glimpse of Alberta's spectacular scenery is offered these pages. A glorious sunset over Medicine Lake, situated in Jasper National Park in the Rocky Mountains, is shown left; while the same lake has a totally different charm in daylight hours when blue skies are reflected in its waters and the snow can be seen clinging to the distant peaks opposite page below. In serene mood bottom, Medicine Lake lies deep, blue and mysterious, hiding who-knows-what secrets? The Athabasca River below presented the pioneer travelers with all manner of hazards, including the Athabasca Falls right.

ALBERTA

Of the many different species of wildlife inhabiting the Rockies these pages, the mountain goats and bighorn sheep favor the high alpine areas, and elk and deer prefer the lush forest meadows. Chipmunks, ground-squirrels and coyotes are not so particular about where they feed.

Banff National Park, comprising 2,564 square miles of peaks and glaciers, alpine meadows, forested slopes, rivers and lakes, is a wildlife paradise. The park's museum introduces the visitor to its many birds and animals which include beaver, muskrat, elk, mule deer, bighorn sheep and moose.

mountain goats, Columbia ground squirrels, chipmunks, and the hoary marmot, whose long shrill whistle, rather like that of a policeman, is one of Jasper's many sounds. Almost never sighted is the small herd of mountain caribou that range the headwaters of emerald-green Maligne Lake. In fall, the distant, resonant bugle of bull elk announces the beginnings of the autumn rut to all the park.

Jasper in winter is superb skiing and long evenings in cosy chalets listening to the mournful, deep-throated howl of the park's wolves resounding through the still, snow-laden firs.

Far to the southwest is Waterton Lakes National Park. Its southern boundary is the international border. On the American side is Glacier National Park. The two parks were joined together in 1932 by acts of the Canadian Parliament and the American Congress to form the unique Waterton-Glacier International Peace Park. An area of mountains, lakes and abundant wildlife, it is a favorite with hikers and campers.

Howls and "yahoos" fill the air in Calgary each July. No, it is not wolves, it is the cowpokes who gather here for the ten days of broncobusting, wild-horse racing, calf wrestling, and buffalo riding that are some of the main events of the annual Calgary Stampede. Highlight of the Stampede is a peculiarly Albertan event – chuckwagon racing. Picture four covered chuckwagons, twenty riders, and a total of thirty-two horses, all churning up dust in a mad dash for a single point on a long dirt track and you have chuckwagon racing, a wild reminder of Alberta's vital cattle industry.

Prime Alberta beef is as popular with Canadians as Alberta oil. Like the oil industry, Alberta's rich cattle industry owes its beginnings to her American neighbors. In 1877 an American drove some cattle over the border looking for a buyer. He found one in a Constable Whitney of the North West Mounted Police (the predecessors of the Royal Canadian Mounted Police), who turned the animals out to graze on the prairie. They not only survived, but multiplied. Word got around, and soon other Montana- and Wyoming-bred herds were being driven north by American cowboys. The government was more than happy to lease great tracts of the western prairies to these new ranchers, and to the retired Mounties who were to swell their ranks.

Today, the foothills country of southwestern Alberta contains some of the finest grazing land in Canada. Here where the flat prairies slowly merge with the Porcupine Hills as they build up toward the Rockies, grasses cure on the stalk, producing a sweet, natural hay. Winter chinooks – warm dry winds from the west – descend from the Rockies, melting temporarily winter's snowy grasp on the land, thereby enabling livestock to graze on pasture vegetation.

Although the first Albertan herds were Texan Longhorns, most herds today are made up of Herefords, often crossbred with exotic European breeds like Charolais, Limousins, and Simmentals. However, long

The animals of the Rocky Mountains these pages are a fascinating mixture of prairie, forest, and arctic creatures. Each has its own environ- *mental requirements and can only survive where these exist.*
Overleaf *A pulp and paper mill.*

ALBERTA

before Montana cowpokes ever cracked their whips to bring straying "little doggies" into line, this land and much of the prairies was the preserve of vast herds of buffalo and of the Blackfoot, Cree, Shoshoni, Piegans and Bloods Indian tribes who hunted them. There are over 10,000 prehistoric sites in Alberta, some indicating that perhaps Alberta's first citizens may have hunted in this land more than 40,000 years ago.

Before Europeans brought guns to the prairies, Indians killed the buffalo by stampeding the herds over steep cliffs known as "buffalo jumps." Old Woman's Buffalo Jump, just south of the pleasant foothills town of High River, is believed to be 1,500 years old. The Head-Smashed-In Jump (now a historical site), west of Lethbridge, is the oldest jump in the prairies. At the bottom of the cliff, a layer of buffalo bones some twelve feet thick are the remains of countless buffalo killed here from 3700 B.C. to the nineteenth century.

Lethbridge itself is Alberta's third largest city, and an important meat-packing and grain-distribution center. Once called Coalbanks, because of the coal seams first worked here in 1870, Lethbridge is, thanks to vast

The sparkling waterfalls above make up part of the Athabasca Falls found in Jasper National Park in the Rocky Mountains. In the background can be seen Fryatt Mountain, which reaches a height of 11,026 feet. Two views of the Athabasca River can be seen right and above right, while facing page is a shimmering view of the Columbia Icefield. Jasper National Park, established in 1907, was named after Jasper House, a trading post set up by Jasper Hawes of the North West Company. The passes and valleys of the park were, however, explored long before 1907 – first by the fur traders, then by the railroad surveyors, geologists, botanists and mountaineers. Today there are more than 600 miles of hiking trails leading down through tranquil valleys, past deep blue lakes and up to remote, wind-swept ridges of high land. Besides hiking, favorite pastimes in this lovely park are fishing and photography.

Banff National Park these pages began as a 10-square-mile preserve around the Sulphur Mountain hot springs near the town of Banff. Since then the park, still famous for its springs, has grown to cover a staggering 2,564 square miles. Banff is Canada's oldest national park, established in 1885. It is a well-known skiing center, and canoeing and horseback riding are other popular activities. One of the prettiest sights in the park is Lake Louise in the snow below, below left and opposite page bottom. Hikers have a wide range of trails to choose from, each of which follows a path through spectacularly lovely and varied countryside.

Overleaf The attractive resort of Banff seen from Mount Norquay, and showing Mount Rundle to the left.

rrigation, the center of a thriving agricultural region.

The buffalo could only survive as long as the old raditional life on the plains remained. The increasing number of white hunters, the ready availability of firearms o the Indians, and a growing demand for buffalo meat and hide brought about their demise. By 1880 the buffalo were gone. Of the once mighty herds that thundered across the prairies, some 1,500 survivors were relocated in Wood Buffalo National Park in 1922. This enormous park, the world's largest, straddles the Alberta-Northwest Territories border and is a haven not only for the buffalo, now numbering around 12,000 animals, but also for the one hundred or so whooping cranes who nest here each summer.

Contact with the Europeans brought disaster to the Plains Indians. Whiskey and European diseases ravaged their number. An inability to appreciate the European attitude to personal land ownership and the careless exploitation of natural resources left the Indians with no place in the emerging frontier society of the prairies. They retired to reservations, today still administered by the federal government.

The eerie, wild and windswept Red Deer Badlands in easterncentral Alberta have long eluded the human hand of progress, but nature has been fashioning these weathered bluffs, bizarre hoodoos, or rock pillars, and deep-trenched gullies for millions of years. Standing in this sunbaked, rocky, barren land it's hard to believe that

ALBERTA

once it was a lush world of magnolias, sycamores and swampy forests where dinosaurs lived. This strange world can be imagined through a visit to Dinosaur Provincial Park at Drumheller, a prosperous grain town.

While furs and cattle brought some Europeans to Alberta, homesteading was responsible for the settlement of the province. Although the railway, laid across Alberta in an amazing eight months during 1882-83, was meant to

The still, calm waters of First Vermilion Lake, and the little boats moored to the jetty opposite page, are a positive invitation to anyone wishing to get away from it all. Moraine Lake below left, also situated in Banff National Park, opens the gateway to the Canadian Rockies from the west. Peyto Lake, a stretch of silky water surrounded by forest-clad slopes and ice-capped peaks, is pictured bottom. Banff Golf Course below *proves an irresistible temptation to golfers from all over the world.*

bring settlers flooding in from eastern Canada, the first homesteaders were Mormons who came north from Utah by wagon train in 1887. These forty families settled in the southwest corner, calling their community Cardston in honor of their leader Charles Card, a son-in-law of Brigham Young.

Settlers from eastern Canada and Europe soon followed: Germans, Ukrainians, French-Canadians, Ontarians, Norwegians from the Dakotas, and peaceful Hutterites. (Some 6,000 Hutterites, members of an old sixteenth-century religious sect, live in central Alberta today. Speaking an old German dialect and dressing in the subdued garb of their forebears, the Hutterites hold their land in common, farming it collectively.)

Between 1885 and 1901, Alberta's population doubled, thanks to the persistent campaign of the federal government to attract settlers from Europe and the United States to the Canadian West. By 1906, the year after Alberta gained formal provincial status, the population had doubled again, topping 150,000.

The homesteader's life was not easy, with fire, grasshoppers, mosquitoes, hailstorms, blizzards, rain and drought all taking their turn to plague the settlers. Neighbors were far away and the isolation was hard to bear, especially in winter. But for those with the fortitude to hang on and clear the required ten to fifteen acres a year, free title to 160 acres was guaranteed at the end of three years.

Today, twenty-seven million acres of Alberta's fifty million acres of land suitable for agriculture are under cultivation. Hogs, dairy cattle, and sheep are raised in addition to beef. Irrigation has meant an expanding vegetable and corn crop, and the growth of specialty crops like sugar beet. Grain, in particular wheat, barley, oats, rapeseed, rye, and flax, is grown on farms across Alberta, and is vital to Alberta's – and Canada's – economy.

Life is very good in Alberta. Sleek cattle graze the prairies; golden grain ripens everywhere under the strong summer suns; tourists play happily in the Rockies; and oil flows twenty-four hours a day, enriching the province's treasury. Winters are cold, but thanks to the chinooks, quite bearable.

Albertans, by temperament a generous, hospitable, outgoing people, quick to help and slow to criticize, enjoy their good fortune with gusto. Still, the dark days of the Depression when howling dust storms swept away the dreams of countless Alberta homesteaders, and bread-lines snaked through Edmonton, are too much a part of local folklore to allow Albertans to squander their new-found wealth. Thanks to the province's Heritage Fund, created from Alberta's oil revenues, a secure, diversified economic structure is being put in place in Alberta against the day when her oil wells run dry.

There is no doubt about it, Canada's youngest province, just now entering her prime, is headed for a golden future.

Farming is one of Alberta's richest industries. The first attempt at cultivating the province's soil was back in 1779, when a certain Peter Pond planted a small garden near Lake Athabasca. This picture facing page top *gives an idea of the progress of agriculture since then! Ponoka* facing page below left *lies on Alberta Number 2 highway, which passes the rapeseed fields of Fairview* top left *and through the farmlands around Beaverlodge* left.

SASKATCHEWAN

People who have come to know Canadians in different regions of the country are agreed: Prairie folk have a personality all their own. Perhaps because Saskatchewan is more typically prairie than Manitoba or Alberta, Saskatchewanians also typify the prairie personality best. They are independent, optimistic, and as tenacious a people as can be found anywhere. Visitors who expect to find picturesque rustics in Saskatchewan (it contains almost half of the country's productive farmland) are in for a surprise; Saskatchewanians are innovators – always have been. And the single trait most indicative of their innovative spirit is their co-operative approach to life.

All over Saskatchewan there are "co-ops": co-operative retail stores, producer co-operatives, credit unions – all returning good old-fashioned profits to participating members. In fact, since 1944, when a socialist government came to power in Saskatchewan, the whole province has been a kind of people's co-op.

In 1932, M.J. Coldwell and J.S. Woodsworth forged a union between Saskatchewan's farmers and laborers to create a new political entity, the Co-operative Commonwealth Federation, or C.C.F., which later became the New Democratic Party.

Just eleven years after the C.C.F's founding convention the party won provincial power, making it the first socialist government in North America, and it has held power almost continuously ever since. Though its offspring, the N.D.P., has never won federal power, the general popularity of many of its party platforms has had a great influence on Canadian society, reflected in Canada's national approach to health, welfare, education and resource development.

Innovation and co-operation have been essential elements in Saskatchewan's corporate soul from the very beginning. In pioneering days, farmers helped each other to break the tough prairie sod, build their log or sod houses, dig wells, plant and harvest crops. They nursed each other through sickness and shared the awful burdens of poverty and isolation. Whatever trials the settlers had suffered in leaving their homes across the cold Atlantic, in eastern Canada or in the United States, there were many more to face when they reached the Red River, the gateway to the free lands in the North West Territories. Land was free all right – just a $10 registration fee and a promise to break the sod were needed to qualify – but getting there was expensive. Passenger and freight rates by water were $230 per head and 14¢ per pound from Fort Garry (now Winnipeg) to Prince Albert, the site of early settlement in Saskatchewan Territory's fertile park belt, near the geographic center of the province. Those who could not afford to go by water could buy a double wagon for $75, but even that was too much for most settlers. On the other hand almost everyone could afford a Red River Cart, a yoke and an ox, which when combined made an unbeatable machine for transporting heavy loads for long distances. The Métis, the children of Indian and white parents who were the west's first settlers, invented it to facilitate buffalo hunting. A Red River Cart was made entirely of wood, with parts joined by pegs or bound together with rawhide strips. It had a hardwood axle which needed no grease and could be repaired with a jackknife, and two huge spoked wheels – over six feet high – which could be removed to convert the cart into a

Watering Saskatchewan's huge fields is no easy task facing page top right, *but carefully designed sprinkler systems make the work look simple! It is hard to imagine nowadays, but once upon a time great herds of buffalo thundered over these fertile agricultural plains. They were wiped out by mass slaughter, and the bison's old domaine became Canada's bread-basket. Saskatchewan has nearly half the nation's farmland and grows two-thirds of its wheat. It is a province of small towns and has only eight cities with a population of 10,000 or more. In the north, there are lakes, rivers, birch and pine woods – a camper's paradise – and for canoeists there are 55 different marked water runs, of varying degrees of difficulty. Back in the south, grain elevators left are the so-called "treasuries for Saskatchewan gold", and they dominate the skyline of the Canadian wheat belt.*
Overleaf An electric storm passes over Halkett Lake in the Prince Albert National Park.

raft. It was light, fast, it would carry a ton of freight, and best of all it was dirt cheap, just $15 in the 1870s.

Once the aspiring farmers reached the settlement lands, they needed about a thousand dollars to set themselves up properly. Few of them had any such fortune, so they relied on working in lumber camps, as laborers for the more affluent settlers or, later, for the railway companies. Most settlers were young bachelors. Two or three would get together and share a shack or sod house and put in a garden: It was critical to grow enough vegetables to eat, with some left over to sell to help buy sugar, salt, flour, clothes and medicines.

In the beginning most of the homesteaders came singly or, at most, as a family. When the railroads came in the 1880s and 1890s, they made it possible for whole groups of settlers to come – individuals bound together by a common ideal, or a religion, or a need to escape a bad political or economic climate in their countries of origin. Colonization societies were organized, and slowly the territory's population grew. To the Fort Qu'Appelle area, in

SASKATCHEWAN

southeastern Saskatchewan, came a colony of British settlers who set to work transforming the old fur fort into an orderly agricultural community. Near Qu'Appelle, Swedes founded the town of Stockholm, and Icelandic colonies set themselves up in the Yorkton area, some miles to the north. Russian Mennonites moved into the Rosthern district, mid-way between Prince Albert and Saskatoon. Under the auspices of Count Paul d'Esterhazy, a colony of Hungarians put down roots in Esterhazy, Whitewood and Kaposvar, north of the Qu'Appelle Valley. Baron de Hirsch brought Jewish refugees to Oxbow, Wapella and Hirsch.

Saskatchewan's livestock industry is very important. The land of wide horizons or "big sky country" stretches from the border of the United States to the North West Territories. Until entering Confederation in 1905, the province in fact formed part of the North West Territories. Under broad skies lie virgin grasslands, wilderness forests and rich fields of grain. Saskatchewan's plains are governed by unruly weather, a climate of stark contrasts. In the summer, temperatures may soar to 110°F, and in the winter fall to 50 below zero! Strong swirling winds, drought and torrential rains all have to be contended with, as do thick swarms of mosquitoes and midges which throng the wooded areas and plague both people and livestock. Despite all this, however – or perhaps because of it – the residents of this province are down to earth and stoical, putting up with the unpredictability of the weather, and taking pride in their land.

A Rumanian colony settled in the Regina area in 1891, which had by then been proclaimed the capital of Saskatchewan Territory. Sponsored by both the renowned author, Count Leo Tolstoy, and English Quakers, three large colonies of Doukhobors settled near Yorkton and Prince Albert. There were colonies of Germans, Danes, French from France and Quebec. Groups of Ontarians and Americans came. Ukrainians, courted by Canada's immigration minister who believed them to be ideal settlers because of their knowledge of dryland farming, came, and, indeed, proved to be an incalculable asset.

In 1873 the North West Mounted Police was created to control the trappers and whiskey traders preying on the Indians, and to ward off a general uprising of Indian tribes made desperate by the disappearance of the buffalo and the destruction of their old way of life. After their long trek from the east, the Mounties set up their posts at the present sites of Battleford and Regina, and in many other places in the North West Territories. By fair dealing, fearlessness, and service, they won the respect of Indians and settlers alike – though no one could change the depressing picture for the Indians and Métis. The Métis, having been pushed out of the Red River area in Manitoba when the authorities insisted on the square-lot survey system and denied them title to their long, narrow, riverfront strip-farms, had moved into Saskatchewan around Duck Lake and Batoche. Then, when the railroad reached the prairies, government surveyors again moved in to lay out townships and square-lot homesteads, and again the Métis were denied title to their farms. Led by

Louis Riel and Gabriel Dumont, and joined by Cree tribes under the legendary chiefs Big Bear and Poundmaker, the ancestral peoples rebelled – only to be defeated in 1885 by a force that outnumbered them five to one.

By 1900 the North West Mounted Police had established the Queen's law throughout the territory, becoming in the process, the stuff of legends. The exploits of the scarlet-jacketed Mounties are known around the world.

Between 1901 and 1917, the population of Saskatchewan had more than quintupled. Aided by the territorial administration, farmers organized a network of self-help associations dating from the 1890s, such as the Dairymen's Association and the Western Stockgrowers. Experimental farms were set up to develop new strains of wheat and other grain crops, as well as livestock, trees, vegetables and even flowers. When Saskatchewan Territory became a province within Confederation in 1905, the provincial government built on these foundations.

It seems ironic that a province that today is world famous for the abundance and quality of its wheat crops, and that accounts for over sixty percent of Canada's total wheat production – not to mention forty-five percent of Canada's flax, fifty percent of its rapeseed, and abundant crops of barley, oats and rye – was once thought to be totally unsuitable for settlement. Yet such was the case back in the 1850s when Great Britain, worried about American incursion north of the 49th parallel, funded an expedition led by Captain John Palliser to investigate the potential of the "interior." Palliser's assessment was that

SASKATCHEWAN

the prairie was an arid desert unfit for agriculture.

At the same time Confederation was already in the wind in Canada. The dream of linking all the British North American colonies from the Atlantic to the Pacific meant that the empty regions between would have to be settled. The Canadian government wanted a detailed assessment of the plains' country, and so, shortly after the Palliser expedition got underway, they sent the University of Toronto's Henry Youle Hind and a team of scientists to explore every aspect of the prairie lands. Hind's assessment of Saskatchewan's agricultural possibilities was more positive than Palliser's, but even he had reservations about the drylands. Yet locked inside those seemingly barren plains was Saskatchewan's fortune.

The road to success was by no means smooth. By sweat of brow and straining muscles the settlers painted the geometric design of farms and towns on the vast canvas of park and prairie, then sent their sons to war in 1914. When the boys got back, the work progressed – until the "dirty thirties." In Saskatchewan the stock-market crash of 1929 was more like the dull thud of the earth's last heartbeat. The disaster of falling prices for farm products was immeasurably compounded by drought and the sickening spectacle of topsoil blowing in the wind like so many molecules of a vanishing dream. Farmers slipped deeper and deeper into debt; mortgages were foreclosed; tens of thousands of farmers were driven from the blighted land. Those who managed to hang on saw prosperity return in the 1940s.

Although agriculture continues to be Saskatchewan's most important industry, it is only one of many. In 1880 George and Sydney Pocock, a couple of would-be buffalo hunters from England found lignite (brown coal) at Roche Percée, a peculiar sandstone formation by the Souris River in the southeastern corner of the province, and Saskatchewan's mining industry was born. Since then, pitchblende containing uranium, copper and zinc has been found and is being exploited. Oil and gas have been discovered near Lloydminster and further south near Swift Current, Estevan, Weyburn and Maple Creek. Today, Saskatchewan is second only to Alberta in the production of these fossil fuels. Oil and gas exploration led to some other lucky finds, among them helium (Saskatchewan is the only commercial source of helium in Canada), sodium sulphate, and most important, potassium, used mainly in fertilizers. Investigation following the initial discovery showed that the extent of this last resource is so vast that the province could supply the world demand for thousands of years into the future!

Water resources? So much talk of drylands and drought is misleading, for Saskatchewan has mighty rivers and literally thousands of lakes. In the north: The historic Churchill River – really a chain of glacial lakes connected by spectacular rapids – flows into Hudson Bay. Huge and majestic Lake Athabasca is part of the Mackenzie system, which empties into the Arctic Ocean. About 250 of the lakes in Saskatchewan's plentiful northern forest support commercial fishing of whitefish, walleye and northern pike, and sportsfishing in the lake country helps to make tourism Saskatchewan's third most

When the pioneers first began to conquer their province, it was a "harsh land of high sky," but in the south, the land is now more gentle and the sweep of rolling prairie is the beloved home of around 100,000 people.

SASKATCHEWAN

important industry. In the south: The fast-flowing waters of the North and South Saskatchewan rivers wind north-eastward across the province, joining at Saskatoon and eventually emptying into Lake Winnipeg, in Manitoba. Further south are the Qu'Appelle, Souris and Assiniboine, which drain into the Red River. There are many lakes in the south, all of which support greenery and outdoor activities. Some are of particular interest. For example, there are hundreds of thousands of "prairie potholes," sloughs created by glaciation which fill with rain and snow or, sometimes, are fed by groundwater full of minerals. Near Swift Current, Little Manitou's mineral content is comparable to that of the Dead Sea, and it has long been a natural health-spa – even before settlement, the Indians called it "the place of healing waters."

In the time-honored tradition of making use of everything, farmers stock the fresh-water potholes on their farms with trout. Whether the prairie potholes contain fresh or salt water, they are oases equally appreciated by wildlife and nature lovers because of the lush vegetation that grows around them.

The other remarkable body of water in southern Saskatchewan is Lake Diefenbaker. In 1958, after years of study, two huge dams were built on the South Saskatchewan River, creating a 145-mile-long reservoir, subsequently named after Saskatchewan's John Diefenbaker, then the Prime Minister of Canada. In addition to creating new sources of hydro-electric power and irrigation, the project has provided a major new recreational resort.

In terms of heavy industry, Saskatchewan's tradition of ingenuity and co-operation has resulted in the creation of an interprovincial steel-making operation. The main complex is located just outside Regina, but there are subsidiary plants in Alberta and British Columbia. The enterprise is part privately owned, part owned by the province. Interestingly, the plants make use of scrap steel from abandoned cars and worn out machinery. Recycling may be considered a follow-through from early days, when settlers had to exploit anything and everything they found around them to live. Huge quantities of buffalo bones strewn over the plains were collected and sold to the United States, where they were transformed into fertilizer. Therefore, it is fitting that Regina was chosen as the site for the steel mill when you consider that the city's first name was "Pile o' Bones" in reference to the sun-blanched relics of the mammoths of the great plains, found there in such eerie abundance.

Other manufacturing ventures include farm machinery, electronics, pulpmills, fish processing and packaging. Handicrafts are produced by an Indian crafts co-operative, that like the Hansen-Ross pottery studio, is located at Fort Qu'Appelle in the valley that once inspired the Indian poet, Pauline Johnson, and gave refuge to the Sioux fleeing north after the Battle of the Little Big Horn.

All of these are among the resources and enterprises that ensure the continuing prosperity and growth of Saskatchewan's pleasant cities. Although Regina was once dependent on agriculture, its economy has widened, and in the process the former Mounties' outpost has become the "Queen of the Plains." After Regina was named the capital in 1905, Wascana Creek was dammed to make a lake, and a park was created in the heart of the city. Today, Wascana Centre is a scenic green oasis, ideal for

Regina these pages *has been the capital of Saskatchewan since 1905 – having originated as a settlement called "Pile o' Bones"! The new City Hall* below and bottom *was opened in 1977; the elegant Legislative Building* facing page top and bottom *stands in a 2,000-acre parkland in the heart of the city – the Wascana Centre.*

cycling, boating, or strolling amid the formal gardens and fountains that grace the lawns between the Legislative Building and the University of Regina, both located there.

Saskatoon, the province's second largest city, is a manufacturing and distribution center – and a far cry from its origin as a temperance colony started by teetotalers from Ontario in 1883. The city's lovely tree-lined streets and numerous parks, its steepled churches, and graceful bridges spanning the South Saskatchewan River which

runs through its center do credit to its residents. In 1971 Saskatoon hosted the Canadian Winter Games. Mount Blackstrap, Canada's highest man-made mountain (300 feet) was built for the occasion, and today the people enjoy excellent downhill skiing.

A big bend in the Moose Jaw River shaped like a moose's jaw may account for the name of the industrial city of Moose Jaw, or the name may have come from the Indian word *moosgaw,* meaning "warm breezes." The city is definitely warmer in winter than the surrounding countryside, and it is cooler in the summer when residents and visitors throng to the Moose Jaw Wild Animal Park, featuring animals from all over the world.

In fact, just about every city and town in Saskatchewan – whether it be Swift Current, Yorkton, North Battleford (across the North Saskatchewan River from historic Battleford, capital of the territory from 1877 to 1883) or Maple Creek – has been shaped to enrich the community life of the province.

And when you consider the hardships, the work, and the sheer inventiveness it took to do it – that is saying a lot!

MANITOBA

For most Canadians, the west begins on the corner of Portage Avenue and Main Street, in Winnipeg, Manitoba. Whether this view is correct geographically matters little. Where these two streets cross is seen as the symbolic departure point of the pioneers whose struggles turned the vast Canadian west into one of the great granaries of the world.

In many ways, modern multi-cultured Canada was born in this community on the Red River. And standing on the corner of Portage and Main, especially on one of those bright, frigid Manitoba winter days, enables one to imagine, just a little, the feelings of fear and hope of all those countless Scots, Irish, English, Swedes, Galicians, Austrians, Germans, Russians, French, Icelanders, Americans, Jews, Ukrainians, and Poles who once briefly stood here, too, fingers and toes quickly numbing in the sub-zero temperature.

European settlement in Manitoba only began in the early years of the nineteenth century when Scottish crofters migrated to the Red River Valley. The Scots, however, were not the first Europeans to come to this land. Two hundred years before, in 1610, Henry Hudson had claimed the great northern bay that bears his name for England. Two years later, the British explorers, Thomas Button and Francis Nelson, also reached Hudson Bay.

Gazing across the surging shoal waters at the ragged shores and rocky crests of the bay's west coast, Button and Nelson realized with bitter disappointment that they, too, had failed to find the Northwest Passage to the Orient which they had been seeking. Wintering in the bay, Nelson and most of his crew died of cold, hunger, and scurvy. With spring, Button and the surviving crew limped back to Britain where Button was able to tell tales of abundant furred animals, whose luxurious pelts far surpassed those of European creatures.

The capital of Manitoba is Winnipeg these pages and overleaf, *which has attracted a wealth and variety of culture, entertainment and business. The Manitoba Legislature* right *was built between 1913 and 1919, in classical Greek style. On top of its dome is the famous Golden Boy, a gilded bronze statue of a running youth. At the base of the elegant marble staircase, which leads from the vestibule to the antehall* facing page below, *are two vast bronze buffaloes – emblems of Manitoba.*

Further expeditions confirmed these rumors of northern riches and inspired a group of English noblemen to form the Company of Gentlemen Adventurers Trading into Hudson Bay. Petitioning Charles II for unlimited rights to the region, the company was granted title to all the land drained by the rivers that flow into Hudson Bay, some one-and-a-half-million square miles. They named this land Rupert's Land, in honor of the king's cousin and the chief financier of the group. With such a monopoly, the Hudson's Bay Company had but to build forts and trading posts, or factories, at the bay and wait for the Indians to come to them with pelts, which were exchanged for rum and blankets and other trade goods.

But while the British sat complacently in their forts, and the company's proprietors counted out their money at home in London, the enterprising French were establishing a chain of fur forts northwest from the Great Lakes to the plains country. Winnipeg, the future capital of Manitoba, was to rise on the site of one of these fur forts, Fort Rouge, built in 1739 at the fork of the Red and Assiniboine rivers.

With the English conquest of Quebec in 1749 control

The Manitoba Museum of Man and Nature facing page top is one of Canada's finest interpretive museums. The visitor is invited to travel in time – and look at the oceans as they appeared four million years ago, and the now fossilized creatures which inhabited them; or visit the waterfront in seventeenth century England where a two-masted ship awaits high tide. Absorb the atmosphere of a young western city in the first successful flush of youth at the turn of this century; and relive the thrilling excitement of a Red River buffalo hunt as the echo of a thousand hoofs thunders over the distant horizons. At this museum you can explore the past, investigate the world we live in now, and the world which we may be living in tomorrow.

of the French fur trade passed to the new English-speaking merchants of Montreal. By 1783, these Montreal-based merchants, trading as the North West Company, were pressing hard on the Hudson's Bay Company's monopoly.

In the ever-widening quest for furs, Peter Pond of the North West Company discovered Lake Athabasca and Great Slave Lake, Alexander Mackenzie charted the great river that bears his name and went on to cross the Rocky Mountains, while David Thompson, Canada's greatest geographer, mapped the mighty Columbia River. For the Hudson's Bay Company, Henry Kelsey first saw the great plains southwest of Hudson Bay; Anthony Henday travelled west as far as the Red Deer region of Alberta, and Samuel Hearne became the first white man to reach the Arctic Ocean by land.

The children of the fur traders and their Indian wives were known as Métis. They looked upon the west as their home. Here they cultivated their long, narrow strip farms along the rivers and streams of southern Manitoba, hunted buffalo, and worked for the large fur-trading companies as their fathers did before them. This idyllic life came to an end in 1811 with the arrival of the first Scottish settlers at Fort Garry.

Abused by their highland chiefs who turned them off their farms in order to raise sheep, Scotland's landless poor at the turn of the nineteenth century had no future but

starvation. Their plight moved Lord Selkirk, a Scottish philanthropist. Hearing of the vast emptiness of the Canadian plains, Selkirk proposed transplanting his land-hungry countrymen to Canada, in particular, to southern Manitoba. Buying the controlling interest in the Hudson's Bay Company (with the Napoleonic Wars having temporarily ruined the market for furs in Europe, shares in the company fell from £250 to £60), Selkirk then dispatched his first fleet of homeless Celts to Manitoba. They arrived in the fall and wintered at York Factory, at the foot of Hudson Bay. Those who survived that first winter then had to make their way by canoe and on foot 750 miles south by way of the Nelson River, Lake Winnipeg, and, finally, the Red River to its confluence with the Assiniboine. Here in the promised land of the Red River Valley, their true nightmare began.

With only hoes and spades to turn the untilled soil of the plains, the Selkirk settlers were unable to raise sufficient crops to feed themselves. To starvation was added constant raids by marauding bands of Métis and Nor'Westers, who rightfully surmised that settlement and fur trade were incompatible.

With nothing to go back to, the Red River settlers hung on tenaciously. In time, the settlement expanded as retired Hudson's Bay factors took to farming along the river. The company's Fort Garry was the administrative center of the settlement, although trade was carried on in the little village of Winnipeg, which sheltered in the protection of the fort. Ten years after the Selkirk settlers arrived in the valley, a hardy group of French Canadians settled opposite Fort Garry in St. Boniface, and together French and Scots braved floods, plagues of grasshoppers, scorching summer heats, fierce blizzards, and crop-flattening hailstones.

Such government as there was in the valley was administered by the Hudson's Bay Company through the Council of Assiniboia. Although cut off from the rest of Canada by thousands of miles of wilderness, the Red River settlement was far from being a cultural wasteland. The occasional visitor arriving up the Red River from the United States noted the churches and schools the settlers had built, and admired the graceful dancing of the ladies and the spirited conversation to be found in Red River's tiny parlors. Dickens was highly popular in the valley, and copies of the *London Illustrated News*, which reached the settlers from Hudson Bay, were passed from hand to hand and read with great interest.

But isolation from the rest of Britain's colonies in Canada was coming to an end. In 1867, Upper and Lower Canada (Ontario and Quebec) joined with Nova Scotia and New Brunswick in Confederation. With a growing population, the new Dominion of Canada was eager for land, and greedily eyed the western territory of the Hudson's Bay Company, still known as Rupert's Land. The following year, the Company agreed to sell Rupert's Land to Canada.

In this aerial view of Winnipeg left *can be seen the Manitoba Legislature Building, its dome topped by the famous Golden Boy statue. The city is situated at the confluence of the Red and Assiniboine rivers, 60 miles north of the Minnesota border of the United States. The name of the city is derived from the Cree Indian words "win nipee" meaning "muddy water." The city is now the main grain market place of the Prairie provinces.*

MANITOBA

The Métis, under their leader, Louis Riel, opposed this flagrant sale of their homes and their birthright, and in November 1869, seized the Hudson's Bay Company post at Lower Fort Garry. Alarmed, the government of Sir John A. Macdonald, Canada's first prime minister, promised the Métis land and the right to educate their children in French. This agreement assured the creation of the province of Manitoba (named for the great Indian spirit, Manitou), which officially came into being on May 12, 1870.

It is one of the more shameful blots on Canadian history that all the promises made to the Métis were broken. And as a new wave of Canadian settlers made their way into Manitoba, the dispossessed and bitter Métis were pushed further westward, settling around Batoche on the banks of the South Saskatchewan River in Saskatchewan. Here in 1885, Riel was to lead them and their Indian allies in their last stand. The Métis were defeated: Riel was captured, tried and hanged for treason.

At his trial, Riel made an impassioned plea for the rights of minorities, a plea that would often go unheeded in the future when immigrants from across the world began to arrive in Manitoba, and later in the other provinces of the west.

Not surprisingly, though, the first of the new wave of settlers to come to Manitoba were not from overseas, but from Ontario. The Canadians were followed by the covered wagons, or prairie schooners as they were known, of American farmers unhappy with conditions in the western United States.

Persecution under Tzarist Russia led 7,500 German-speaking Mennonites to depart their homeland for

The Winnipeg Mint above is a branch of the Royal Canadian Mint, the most modern in the world. It was designed so that the general public could see the exciting processes that go into money-making, including 32 coin presses which transform blanks into coins at a speed of 300 strokes a minute! In spring and summer, visitors enjoy paddle-steamer cruises above right up and down the Red and Assiniboine rivers. The Viking statue facing page was photographed at Gimli on Lake Winnipeg, while pictured right is a pretty little rural church near Morden.

Overleaf Clear Lake is found in Riding Mountain National Park. The mountain itself is part of the Manitoba Escarpment, a jagged ridge that winds across North Dakota, Manitoba and Saskatchewan.

MANITOBA

Manitoba, arriving in 1874. The following year brought 1,250 Icelanders to the province, where they settled at Gimli (meaning the Great Hall of Heaven) on Lake Winnipeg. Swiss and Swedes came next, the latter by way of the United States. Hungarians, Czechs, Slovaks and Britons also made their way to Manitoba and points further west during the 1870s and 1880s. The bloody pogroms of the early 1880s led a small group of Jews to leave Russia. With help from their brethren already in Canada, they arrived in Manitoba in 1882.

By 1881 the railway reached Winnipeg. Yet the expected flood of new settlers was slow in starting. Over a decade would pass before a Winnipeg businessman, Clifford Sifton, serving as Minister of the Interior in the government of Sir Wilfrid Laurier, instituted a concerted campaign to woo immigrants to Manitoba and the west. Mounting a massive advertising blitz, Sifton dispatched his staff to set up immigration offices in Great Britain and Ireland, and the western United States. Successful farmers already established in the west were recruited for service abroad, where they addressed prospective settlers on the merits of farming in the west.

"Fruitful Manitoba – the best wheat land and the richest grazing land under the sun . . ." ran the cover of one handsome pamphlet, soon translated into French, German, Russian, Italian, Ukrainian, and other European languages. And from the squalid industrial cities of England and the wild steppes of the Ukraine, from the terraced valleys of the Rhine and the craggy fjords of Scandinavia, the people, yearning for land of their own, answered Sifton's call. Selling their few belongings to raise their passage, they journeyed steerage across the rough Atlantic. From Montreal or Halifax, weary and bedraggled, they were jammed aboard crowded "colonist cars" for the long rail trek to the land of milk and honey.

For many, Winnipeg was to be the end of the line. Too exhausted and too broke to go any further, they trudged north up Main Street from the rail depot, stopped to catch their breath where Portage Avenue crosses Main, and then disappeared into the burgeoning slums of the city's north end. Others, more fortunate, perhaps, took the train deep into the heart of Manitoba, alighting at tiny sidings to claim their portion of the "Last Best West."

But what type of land was it that awaited Mr. Sifton's "stalwart peasants in sheepskin coats?"

Once, countless years ago, most of what is now Manitoba was covered by a vast freshwater lake, known to geologists as Lake Agazziz. Over seven hundred miles long and two hundred and fifty miles wide, this lake is believed to have formed and disappeared four times as the glaciers of the great ice ages advanced and retreated. Although the original lake is gone forever, it bequeathed to Manitoba Lakes Winnipeg, Manitoba, and Winnipegosis, not to mention the myriad tiny lakes that cause mapmakers to speckle much of Manitoba blue. Lake Agazziz also left Manitobans the vital Red and Nelson rivers. But perhaps the greatest legacy of the bygone lake is the thick deposit of silt and clay that covered its enormous bottom. It was here on the bottom of old Lake Agazziz that prairie homesteaders were to build their farms and realize their dreams.

Manitoba...gentle rolling farmlands inhabited by exceptionally friendly and hospitable people.

This triangular-shaped land of rich plains makes up most of southern Manitoba. Wheat, rapeseed, barley, oats, triticale, tame hay, and flax grow abundantly well here, as do splendid yellow sunflowers, whose massed heavy heads turn Manitoba's late-summer fields into a blaze of golden glory. Complementing the plains are gentle wood-covered hills and pastoral valleys.

Starting at the eastern shore of Lake Winnipeg and sweeping north all the way to the sixtieth parallel, lies the ruggedly beautiful country of the great Canadian Shield.

In addition to the vastness of their new land, settlers also had to come to terms with a climate not at all like the balmy clime mentioned in Sifton's pamphlets. Bitterly cold winters turned out to be the rule not the exception, and spring brought either too much rain, which turned the soil into mud, or gumbo, defying horse, man, and plough, or no rain at all, causing the rapidly warming sun to bake the soil rock hard.

Perhaps the most successful settlers were the Ukrainians and the Mennonites, who were used to farming the cold Russian steppes. But for them, as for all other homesteaders, success was bought at great cost. The brave letters and fading photos of the period tell of perishing winters spent huddled in one-room sod huts, of isolation and loneliness, of tiny white coffins and exhausted women doing the duty of plough horses, of insufficient food, and the round-the-clock work of planting and harvesting and tending to precious stock.

But these Manitoba pioneers, like the Selkirk settlers before them, were a hardy bunch. They not only wrested a living from the land, but also breathed life into Manitoba's towns. Today, nothing better reflects the mosaic of Canadian life than the distinct communities of rural Manitoba. And with most of Manitoba's million-plus population living in the plains region of the south, it is easy for a visitor to take to the road to savor the diversity of Manitoba life first-hand.

Consider Dauphin. French by name but decidedly

The people of Manitoba are proud of their past and celebrate it during various local festivals. At Steinbach below, left and facing page below, a reconstructed Mennonite town first settled by Russians in 1874, Pioneer Days are celebrated every July.

Overleaf An aerial view of Winnipeg in the snow.

Ukrainian in character, Dauphin, to the north of Brandon, yearly celebrates the old homeland on the Dnieper with a round of festivities highlighted by a dazzling kaleidoscope of music and dance.

Or Gimli, the largest Icelandic settlement outside Iceland. Men of Gimli still fish the waters of Lake Winnipeg as their great-grandfathers did over a century ago, netting whitefish and walleye and the pride of the province, the Manitoba goldeye. Icelandic is still spoken here, and young people from Gimli often study the history of their people at the University of Manitoba, in Winnipeg.

MANITOBA

The peaceful communal farming practised by the Mennonites lives on around Steinbach, southeast of Winnipeg. Steinbach, today, is a faithful reconstruction, complete with wind-driven grist mill, of the first Mennonite settlement begun here in 1874.

On the Assiniboine River, Brandon's stately old homes tell of the riches the Wheat City has enjoyed as the chief grain-shipping center of the province. Manitoba's second largest city, Brandon epitomizes the province's agricultural base.

And then there is Winnipeg, Canada's fourth largest city and home to more than half of Manitoba's population. Winnipeg is the fruit of the harvest.

The appalling slums that once were the only refuge of so many immigrants have given way to the cosmopolitan city built by their children and grandchildren. The sweat shops and grimy little factories where once the sons and daughters of Galicia and Hungary, Bessarabia and Italy, toiled so long and hard have been replaced by modern industrial plants whose output makes Winnipeg one of Canada's leading manufacturing cities. Preserving a link with the old, old days, Winnipeg is now a major center for the design and manufacture of fur garments.

But Winnipeg is more than just a vital transportation, financial, and commercial center – the Chicago of the North – it is a city rich in ethnic diversity and blessed with a vibrant cultural life that is the envy of many a larger community.

Winnipeg supports the world-renowned Royal Winnipeg Ballet, the nationally acclaimed Manitoba Theatre Centre, the Winnipeg Symphony, and the Manitoba Opera Company, all of which perform a full range of works, from the classics to experimental and new Canadian pieces, at the city's Centennial Centre.

All Manitoba's ethnic groups are represented in Winnipeg, each well served by community organizations, language classes, cultural groups, and newspapers. And on her broad streets, orthodox churches and synagogues coexist in a way never possible in the old world, and only recently so in the new, proving, at last, the validity of Louis Riel's plea for tolerance.

Each summer Winnipeg acknowledges Manitoba's debt to all her enterprising pioneers by hosting a giant multi-nation folk celebration of feasting and dancing.

The pioneer spirit is not dead in Manitoba. It thrives in particular in the northern shield communities of Flin Flon, Thompson, and The Pas; towns known across Canada for their nickel, zinc, and copper mines, and as lumber and trapping centers. Moreover, it is immortalized in the writings of Manitoba's many authors, Margaret Laurence, Gabrielle Roy, Frederick Phillip Grove, and Ernest Thompson Seton, to mention a few.

But for Manitobans, as for all Canadians, the province with its promise of plenty, will be forever symbolized by that corner at Portage and Main – for so long the front door to the golden west.

The multi-colored fields left in their jigsaw puzzle patterns, form part of the 40-acre Mennonite Village Museum at Steinbach. During the annual Pioneer Days ethnic festival, visitors can see grain being ground to flour at the windmill, watch steam-threshing, log-sawing, horse-shoeing, quilt-making and other fascinating skills and occupations which are kept alive here at the museum.

ONTARIO

Ontario, Canada's major English-speaking province, has all the requirements needed for the good life. Her vast northland is covered in dense forests made for the logger's saw. Her extensive mineral output, the highest in Canada, includes copper, zinc, salt, nickel, gold, uranium, and cobalt, and no country in the world has more silver than Ontario. Her giant foundries produce most of Canada's steel, and her factories dominate the nation's industrial scene. Her borders touch four out of five of the Great Lakes, giving her access not only to one-quarter of all the fresh water in the world but also to the St. Lawrence Seaway, one of the mightiest inland water transportation systems on earth. Her eight-and-one-half-million people make Ontario Canada's most populous province. Her citizens, ninety percent of whom live in southern Ontario on just one-sixth of the province's total land area, enjoy the highest standard of living in the country. Her climate in the southwestern section of the province is, by Canadian standards, mild. Her much colder northland experiences the plummeting temperatures and heavy

The graceful bridge facing page top spans the Sioux Narrows, which form part of the vast Lake of the Woods facing page bottom. This "lake" extends across western Ontario and into Manitoba. Southwards it stretches as far as the United States, and it is studded with no fewer than 14,000 islands above and above right.
INCO: International Nickel's mills, smelters and refineries right recover 15 elements, including nickel, copper, gold and silver. The Ontario division's plants make up one of the largest integrated nickel-copper mining and refining complexes in the world, with five concentrators (mills), a copper-nickel separation plant and an iron ore recovery plant.
Overleaf The Soo Locks, part of the St. Lawrence Seaway, were constructed at Sault Ste Marie in order to avoid the rapids where the St. Mary's River leaves Lake Superior to join Lake Huron, and to overcome the 20 foot difference in water levels between the two lakes.

ONTARIO

snowfalls that guarantee a winter wonderland for skiers, while the short, warm summers are made for modern-day wilderness explorers. Her farms, situated mostly in the fertile south, constitute the most intensely developed agricultural region in Canada. And her capital city, Toronto, one of the leading financial centers in North America, is a cosmopolitan metropolis of innovative shopping complexes, fine restaurants, handsome buildings and abundant cultural delights.

Yet just 200 years ago, Great Britain, having wrested what is now Ontario and neighboring Quebec from the French as part of the spoils from the Seven Years' War, seriously wondered whether it might not be better to trade the new territory for the Caribbean island of Guadeloupe. In the end, the British decided to keep Canada, simply because it was the northern flank of their rich American colonies to the south.

At the time the Treaty of Paris put an end to the Seven Years' War in 1763, Europeans had been in Canada for over 150 years. The French under Samuel de Champlain had first explored Ontario early in the seventeenth century. Making allies of the indigenous Huron Indians, the French were soon assured of a steady supply of beaver pelts.

Upper Canada Village facing page and below is located near Morrisburg. The village is a reconstruction of a typical St. Lawrence Valley community of the nineteenth century. About forty buildings were moved from their original sites, where they were due to be inundated by the St. Lawrence Seaway, to create this settlement.

This characteristic Ontario farm left stands near Thunder Bay, the western terminus of the St. Lawrence-Great Lakes waterway. The province has gently rolling countryside in the south, where fields of wheat top, tobacco, soy beans and vegetables above lie side by side with apple orchards and dairy farms. Here, too, are Ontario's important cities; over ninety per cent of the province's population lives in the south.

Overleaf The sun sets over Millbay, Lake Superior.

ONTARIO

Relations between the French and the Hurons were always extremely good. Champlain's soldiers fought alongside the Hurons in their battles with the tribes of the Iroquoian Confederacy, while the Jesuit missionaries under Jean de Brébeuf established missions in the Huron villages.

But tragically, by 1650, disease and repeated Iroquois attacks had almost wiped out the Huron nation. Brébeuf and his brother missionaries were also casualties of the Iroquois wars, suffering torture and death for the faith they tried to implant in the wilderness.

For the next 100 years the woods and waters of Ontario were travelled by *coureurs de bois*, French Canadian woodsmen who journeyed further and further west from Quebec in search of furs. No French settlers were established in Ontario, but when the British began moving northward from the thirteen colonies, the French were forced to build strategically located forts to protect the vital river routes. In 1749 one such fort was erected at the mouth of the Humber River. Fort Toronto was intended to prevent Indian tribes from trading with the British who had built a fortified port on the south shore of Lake Ontario.

The Seven Years' War, often referred to in the United States as the French and Indian War, found France hard pressed to defend the French settlements of Quebec, let alone the vast wilderness that came to be known as

Ontario is a province of variety – both of climate and landscape. Snowbound country areas facing page contrast starkly with the urban scenery of Toronto below and bottom. The most striking feature of Ontario's capital is its massive skyline of tall banks, hotels and office buildings, seen here sparkling with light as a winter's evening draws in.

Overleaf Spanning the St. Lawrence River is the Ogdensburg International Bridge, which crosses over to the United States at Johnstown.

ONTARIO

Ontario. In 1758, the French were forced to destroy Fort Toronto rather than let it fall into English hands. When Governor Vaudreuil surrendered Montreal to the English in 1760, he effectively put an end to the French presence in Ontario.

However, the Treaty of Paris did not bring peace to North America; in a few years the thirteen American colonies revolted against British rule.

But President Washington's United States were not for everyone. By the end of the American Revolution, the trickle of American colonists loyal to the Union Jack who had made their way north to Nova Scotia, New Brunswick, or Quebec had become a flood. The eastern colonies of British North America were sorely pressed by this sudden growth in numbers – Nova Scotia found her population almost doubled overnight, and soon became known to locals and newcomers alike as Nova Scarcity.

As a result, His Majesty's government in Montreal decided to settle some of the new arrivals in the western part of Quebec; that is, present-day Ontario.

The government allotted the Loyalists, as the newcomers were known, land along the Upper St. Lawrence River, around Kingston and the Bay of Quinte, and in the Niagara Peninsula.

Ironically, while these new settlers were staunch in their loyalty to England, they had breathed the heady air of American republicanism too long to be content with the imperial status quo practised in the north. Not slow to profit by her disastrous experiences with the thirteen colonies, Britain acceded to the Loyalist request for more say in the administration of their affairs, creating in the process the distinct provinces of Upper and Lower Canada (Ontario and Quebec respectively).

The government of Upper Canada, headed by Lieutenant-Governor Sir John Graves Simcoe, consisted of a legislative council and a representative assembly that advised the governor, but real power lay in the hands of a small executive council who, along with the lieutenant-governor, answered directly to Britain.

Convinced that the lack of a strong state religion had contributed to the revolt of the American colonies, Britain firmly established the Anglican Church as the religious foundation of Upper Canada, in the process turning over considerable funds and land – known as the Clergy Reserves – to the Church. Lest the settlers object, they were given their land in freehold tenure, as opposed to the old feudal seigneurial land-tenure system in effect in Lower Canada.

From these modest beginnings a unique ethos of small "c" conservatism embodying loyalty to the Crown, respect for the Church, and the inviolability of private property, took root in Ontario, and flourished for well over a century and a half, fading only with the upheavals of World War II.

Toronto by night this page and facing page top *provides the onlooker with some stunning views. The City Hall* right *was opened in 1965. This daringly designed edifice consists of a white dome nestling between two curved towers, of 20 and 27 storeys, and it has been seen by many as the catalyst prompting* Toronto's cultural and construction booms. The city's most impressive structure, however, must surely be the CN Tower, seen in silhouette top right. *In complete contrast, Ottawa's Parliament Buildings contain many magnificent rooms, including the Confederation Hall* facing page bottom.

ONTARIO

Toronto has a range of cuisines as varied as the nationalities of the immigrants who brought them here, and new restaurants and cafés are opening all the time. The city's Yellow Pages list some forty pages of eating establishments, the ethnic categories commencing with Arabian, Armenian and Austrian and ending with Ukrainian and West Indian! The attractive Hazelton Café left and the street cafés facing page top left and right are situated in the smart Yorkville area. A tempting array of food and flowers invites visitors into Fenton's Restaurant below, while the neon signs of a Chinese restaurant facing page below left add a touch of international color to Elizabeth Street. Yonge Street facing page below right is one of Toronto's busiest shopping and dining areas.

Back in the 1790s, however, Governor Simcoe was less interested in setting the future character of Ontario than he was in finding an appropriate site for Upper Canada's capital. Newark (Niagara-on-the-Lake) was, for a brief period, the capital, and Kingston was also considered, but their close proximity to the United States made them too vulnerable to any future American attack. Finally, Simcoe

agreed to the site of the old fur fort on the Humber River, Fort Toronto, which he renamed York.

In 1812, what Simcoe had always feared came to pass – Upper Canada was attacked by the Americans. The United States saw the War of 1812 as a reaffirmation of the Revolution, and determined to remove the British at their back door. Great Britain, preoccupied with fighting

Napoleon in Europe, was hardly aware of events in Canada. Upper Canada, however, was invaded, and in the two years the war lasted, fighting in Upper Canada was fierce, with local farmers standing shoulder to shoulder with the few British troops garrisoned in the colony. York was raided and burnt to the ground.

At war's end, Britain decided to fill Upper Canada's empty spaces to prevent American expansion northward. Free land was offered to English, Irish, and Scots who, due to the upheavals caused by the Industrial Revolution, welcomed the chance to start afresh in the colony. These new settlers meant the end of Upper Canada's days as a fur-trapper's wilderness as more and more trees fell to the settlers' axes, and the centuries-old earth turned beneath their plows.

These newcomers soon grew restless under the oligarchical rule of Upper Canada's first families, known as the Family Compact. Loudest of all the opponents to the Family Compact was William Lyon Mackenzie, a fiery

ONTARIO

Toronto's modern face, epitomized by the sophisticated CN Tower right and New City Hall above, both complements and contrasts with its older face, seen in the Old City Hall above right and in the panoramic view of the city overleaf.

Food shopping in Toronto is a real experience, especially in Kensington Market facing page. Kensington Market, situated in the narrow streets of one of Toronto's older neighborhoods, is a European-style market shared by dozens of nationalities. Jewish, Portuguese, West Indian and Italian shops are all crowded into this densely packed area of cheese markets, butchers and fishmongers, bakeries, vegetable and fruit stalls. The aroma of fresh and exotic foods mingles with the exhaust fumes of the crawling traffic, and sounds of music and shouting fill the electrically charged air. Kensington Market is one of Toronto's most alluring and atmospheric tourist attractions.

little journalist from Scotland. When constitutional reform and responsible government were not forthcoming, a rebellion of some several hundred armed men, with Mackenzie at their head, broke out in Toronto in 1837. (York had been incorporated as the City of Toronto in 1834.)

The rebellion failed, as did more serious insurrections in Lower Canada in 1837 and 1838.

The Colonial Office in Britain became seriously alarmed and Lord Durham was sent out to restore tranquillity to the Canadas. Durham's solution was the amalgamation of Upper and Lower Canada under one government. Further, he proposed that the executive council be responsible to the legislative assembly rather than the Crown.

Britain liked the first suggestion, and under the Act of Union, passed in 1840, Upper and Lower Canada were henceforth known as Canada West and Canada East. The seat of government alternated between Quebec City and Toronto. The granting of responsible government did not please Britain nearly as much.

When the British corn laws which had controlled the entry of foreign grain into Britain and which had favored Canada were repealed in favor of free trade, Canada West found herself shut out of her traditional British market. Casting aside her remembrances of past fights, the colony turned to her neighbor to the south and entered into reciprocal trading arrangements with the United States that were to cause a boom in the colony's agriculture and lumbering. Reciprocity would rise and fall over the succeeding decades, but those first agreements, made in 1854, established a vital commercial link between Ontario and the United States which continues to this day.

Hand in hand with this new-found prosperity came Canada West's great railway boom. With the railways came more settlers to farm the land; work in the woollen, grain, and saw mills; mine for copper, silver, and iron ore; and drill for oil at Petrolia, southwest of London.

It was an age for entrepreneurs: Hart Massey laid the

The city of Toronto these pages is said by its residents to be a pleasure to live in, and the city that was once called "Hogtown" now has a population of some three million. City Hall facing page below is a source of local pride. Its huge forecourt, Nathan Phillips Square is the scene of rock concerts, brass bands and political soap-boxes in the summer, and is frozen over as an ice-rink in winter. The CN Tower above reaches a height of 1,815 feet and five inches, making it the tallest free-standing structure in the world.

foundations for a world-wide farm machinery empire, and an Ulster-born haberdasher named Timothy Eaton turned the selling of pins and pants into one of the largest department store enterprises in North America.

When the new Dominion of Canada was proclaimed on July 1, 1867, there was no doubt that Canada West, now called Ontario, was the keystone of the new nation. Her population of one-and-one-half million far outstripped that of her three partners in Confederation – Quebec (formerly Canada East), Nova Scotia and New Brunswick, and, thanks to reciprocity, more than one-third of Canada's economic activity emanated from Ontario.

ONTARIO

Well over a century later, the situation has not changed much. Ontario's manufacturing industries still account for more than fifty percent of Canada's total output of finished goods and for forty percent of all manufactured goods destined for export. Excluding oil, Ontario produces nearly thirty percent of all Canada's minerals and a good forty percent of all the country's structural materials. Twenty-five percent of the nation's agricultural revenue is earned by Ontario's mixed farms, making the province the most valuable agricultural producer in the country.

Toronto, the heir to muddy little York, exemplifies Ontario's prosperity. It is a well-planned, well-run city of solid wealth, clean streets and law-abiding citizens. For a city of its size – Toronto has a population of about three million – it is remarkably free of the downtown slums that mar comparable North American urban centers. Actually, downtown living is extremely popular in Toronto, and houses in inner city areas are in high demand and priced accordingly.

For most of its life, Toronto was known as Toronto the Good (amongst other things), a reference to the staunch Methodism of the majority of its citizens who abhorred strong drink, frowned on tobacco, and decried all Sunday activities excluding churchgoing and sedate family walks.

The oldest and largest annual exhibition in the world, held on the Canadian National Exhibition Grounds, is called the "Ex" these pages. Held every year for over a century, its displays include a multitude of agricultural and technical exhibits, a large midway and a spectacular water show. Set in front of the Canadian National Exhibition Grounds, on Lake Ontario, is Ontario Place overleaf, a showplace for both the province and the nation.

ONTARIO

Ontario Place right, below right and facing page below *is one of North America's great recreational complexes. It is built on, and over, what was once simply a stretch of Lake Ontario. This brilliant transformation has resulted in 96 acres of man-made islands and space-age buildings on long steel legs, linked by a series of walkways. The white spherical building clearly visible in these photographs is the Cinesphere, one of the most futuristic theaters in the world, which shows technically advanced films projected on to a vast six-storey, curved screen in an auditorium which will hold 800 people. The main pavilion area is built on pods suspended some 40 feet above the water of the lake. They house changing multi-media displays and an excellent restaurant.*

Overleaf *The annual Canadian National Exhibition (the "Ex") is a national institution.*

The post World War II influx of immigrants from all over the world has done much to enliven old Toronto. It is still Toronto the Good inasmuch as her streets may be safely walked at night; her citizens, while not effusive, do seem blessed with a ready grasp of the good manners needed to ensure the peaceful co-existence of so many; and, oh yes, Eaton's, mindful of its founder, still will not sell you a pack of cigarettes!

But Torontonians now take Sunday brunch at sinfully good French restaurants; are not in the least bit fazed at hearing Hungarian spoken on Bloor Street; manipulate chopsticks with ease; think nothing of taking in the latest film offerings from New Delhi; and dance up a storm at the yearly Caribana, the West Indian community's carnival in which the whole city joyfully participates.

Toronto's awesome array of churches have undergone a transformation, too. Many are now mosques or temples, where signs out front give the hours of service in Hindi or Japanese, Korean or Arabic.

Young Toronto goes to school in English, gets immersed in French, and often takes after-school grammar lessons in their parents' native tongue, be it Russian, Hebrew, German, Italian, Portuguese, Czech, Vietnamese, Polish, Chinese, Maltese, Ukrainian, Filipino, Dutch or Urdu.

Toronto's shops, like its restaurants, reflect the

cultural diversity of the city. From the elegant stores and boutiques of Bloor Street to noisy, colorful Kensington Market, its narrow streets jammed with Kosher butchers, West Indian greengrocers, and Portuguese fishmongers; from the world's biggest shopping complex, the Eaton Centre on downtown Yonge Street, a city-block-sized, glass-covered emporium of 300 stores, to the shops in Little Italy on St. Clair Avenue West – there is nothing that cannot be bought in Toronto's shops.

When it comes to the arts, Toronto can hold its own with the great cities of the world. Home of the National Ballet of Canada and the Canadian Opera Company, not to mention a score of other theatrical and artistic groups, avant-garde, traditional, or distinctly Canadian, Toronto's artistic calendar is always over-booked.

Toronto's presence as a vital commercial center is evident in her great banking and insurance towers. The Toronto Stock Exchange, second in importance in North America to the New York Stock Exchange, records the economic health of the country.

Toronto, of course, has its lighter side, and the pin-striped-suited stockbroker by day quite likely trades his

A view of Toronto's famous New City Hall is pictured above *while the city's distinctive skyline is illustrated* facing page. *This skyline, while dominated by the CN Tower, features the* more solid outlines of four of the city's office complexes, skyscrapers which bear the names of Canada's four leading banks.*

Overleaf *The Eaton Centre.*

briefcase after hours for a box of popcorn and a ringside seat at Maple Leaf Gardens, home of the Toronto Maple Leafs hockey team. In winter, hockey is an abiding passion in Toronto, as, indeed, in all of Ontario. Nothing starts a conversation quicker between Ontarians than the current standing of the Maple Leafs. Thanks to the Blue Jays, baseball receives almost as much attention during the summer, while fall is given over to following the football fortunes of the Toronto Argonauts.

While no one denies that Toronto is the hub of Ontario, Torontonians themselves are the first to concede that the city really is only the sum of all the parts of the province. Fortunately for visitors to Ontario, the highways are excellent and far-reaching, and despite the province's large size, it is relatively easy to explore.

"Good things grow in Ontario" runs a jingle of the Ontario Ministry of Agriculture and Food, and nowhere is the truth of this little ditty more evident than in the province's southwestern corner. Here, amidst acres of corn, cucumber patches, and fields of ripening, red tomatoes, quiet little villages snooze contentedly in the warm summer sun. Roadside stalls and "pick-your-own" farms invite on-the-spot sampling of nature's bounty.

Southwest Ontario has its urban face, too, exemplified by cities such as Brantford, where Alexander Graham Bell invented the telephone, and London, whose spacious tree-lined streets, big old houses and unhurried air prove

Toronto, like so many large cities, offers a wide range of shops and marketplaces. It has a sizeable downtown shopping district which extends from Yonge Street to University Avenue, and from King Street north to College Street. Yonge Street in particular is famous for its stores, the most spectacular being Eaton's, which is situated in the new Toronto Eaton Centre these pages. Eaton's is one of Canada's retailing giants, and this magnificent modern complex is its showpiece. Featuring a 300-store glass-domed Galleria stretching down Yonge Street from Dundas to Queen, the Eaton Centre first opened in 1977, and now ranks as one of the finest shopping areas in the world.

that prosperity and tranquillity are not incompatible. Once, slaves from America's south struggled north along the Underground Railway to freedom in this part of Ontario. Chatham was the northern terminus of the railway, and today many of the area's residents are the descendants of those once oppressed people.

Drama of a much lighter vein is enacted each summer at the Stratford Festival. Ontario's yearly theatrical extravaganza brings the world's finest performers together with Canada's leading actors in plays by Shakespeare, Chekhov, Pirandello, Coward, and Canadian playwrights such as Michel Tremblay and George Ryga. Situated on the Avon River (where else!), the Festival is within easy driving distance of Toronto.

If Shakespeare fuels Stratford, the acerbic wit of George Bernard Shaw draws thousands to the annual Shaw Festival held at picturesque Niagara-on-the-Lake. The town is early nineteenth-century Ontario at its prettiest, most of its old houses painstakingly restored.

Commercialism has marred much of the area surrounding Niagara Falls, but up close the falls are still a truly remarkable sight. Every minute of the day, nearly half-a-million tons of water pour over the falls in a roaring, pounding, crashing thunder of unbridled power.

Long the honeymoon capital of the world, Niagara Falls is lovely in the summer when the fall's sparkling sprays rise ethereally into the blue sky above, the bright sun casting dancing shadows on the swollen river. But if you can see Niagara Falls in winter when it is not so crowded, when the somber snow-laden skies crown its ice-covered rocks and frigid sprays, it is not hard to imagine the wild untamed beauty of this land before man and progress arrived to take nature firmly by the hand.

Toronto's dazzling Royal Bank Plaza above features the twin towers of the Royal Bank Building top left and facing page, which are covered with $250,000 in gold leaf. The surreal photograph left shows an office block seen through a curved glass skylight.

Overleaf The Château Laurier, a renowned hotel, stands to the right of the Parliament Buildings in Ottawa.

ONTARIO

A few miles from the falls is the Welland Canal, a part of the St. Lawrence Seaway Authority. Created jointly by Canada and the United States, the seaway operates the vast system of locks and canals that make it possible for ocean-going ships to bypass the rapids of the St. Lawrence River and Niagara Falls to reach all of the Great Lakes.

Eastern Ontario is rich in history: Little Adolphustown, first settled by Loyalists long ago; Kingston, once Ontario's guardian against her American neighbors; and Ottawa, Canada's capital, all have their roots deep in the soil of this part of the province. The one-roomed schoolhouses, whitewashed churches, and stone grist mills of eastern Ontario villages are as faithfully preserved as the stately homes and impressive limestone public buildings of the city of Kingston. The city is the site of the Royal Military College; and, while the college concerns itself with modern technological warfare, the days of muskets and powder and soldiers in tight red jackets are not forgotten here. Old Fort Henry, built between 1832 and 1836, regularly mounts an ear-splitting demonstration of nineteenth century military drill – cannons firing, standards flying, and bugles blaring.

Old Fort Henry these pages stands on a hill protectively overlooking the city of Kingston, Ontario. A massive fortress, Fort Henry was once the principal military stronghold of Upper Canada, and the first line of defense in a war between Canada and the United States ... which never took place! It was built between 1832 and 1836, and has a series of cannon-studded Martello towers, powder magazines, barracks, kitchens and workshops, all of which make up a living museum of the military life, architecture and artifacts of a bygone century. The Fort Henry Guard, trained and uniformed as British troops of 1867, parade every day. Infantry drill and tactics are displayed by these living toy soldiers, and salutes are fired daily using the fort's original muzzle-loading cannon, which was cast in Scotland between 1794 and 1806. Overleaf The Jones Falls Locks on the Rideau Canal which follows a route from Kingston to Ottawa.

Toronto's evening skyline below is dominated by towering commercial complexes. In complete contrast, Casa Loma facing page top is a 98 room mansion which was built between 1911 and 1914 by a Toronto soldier, financier and industrialist. Hidden stairways and secret panels lend an air of mystery more appropriate to a fairy castle. Another "fairy castle" is Ottawa's famous hotel, the Château Laurier below left. Bellevue House left and City Hall facing page below are just two of the City's early landmarks. Bellevue House, a fine villa in Tuscan style, was built in 1838. Once the home of Canada's first Prime Minister, Sir John A. Macdonald, it has been restored and refurbished to its original state. City Hall, constructed between 1843 and 1844, is one of the country's great classical buildings.

Overleaf View of Toronto from the CN Tower.

The best show in the country, however, at least according to Canadians, is to be found about a hundred miles northeast of Kingston in the House of Commons in Ottawa. Here the honorable members of Her Majesty's government do verbal battle with Her Majesty's loyal opposition. The badinage flies fast and furious in the House, often dismaying visitors expecting more sedate political procedures.

Ottawa is a beautiful city. Built on a bluff overlooking the Ottawa River, it combines a dual French/English love of ornate architecture and impressive statuary with North American modernity, in a setting of spacious natural

ONTARIO

The Gothic Houses of Parliament these pages dominate views of the city of Ottawa, Canada's capital. They consist of three buildings roofed with green copper, and the central block is crowned by the 291-foot-tall Peace Tower with its carillon of 53 bells. When Parliament is in session, a white light shines at the top of the tower, while the eternal flame facing page top burns in front of the buildings. On the lawns, the Changing of the Guard is performed daily by the Governor-General's Foot Guards above right and facing page center right and left. Outside Parliament, an officer of the Royal Canadian Mounted Police is always on duty above and right to give help and advice to tourists from all over the world. The Senate Chamber facing page bottom is just one of Parliament's magnificent rooms.
Overleaf The mighty Niagara River plunges over Niagara Falls, unhampered by choking winter snows.

beauty so obviously part of the uncrowded new world. Ottawa is easily bilingual on the streets, in the shops, in the House, at the theater, and in the numerous government departments that employ the bulk of the city's 305,000 citizens.

There are more parks in Ottawa than in any other city in Canada, most of them buried under masses of tulips in the spring. Winters, which are undeniably brisk in Ottawa, find the nation's bureaucrats skating on the frozen Rideau Canal which winds through the city.

When Ontarians tire of all the comforts that come with living in the province's cities, they get away from it all in the province's rugged north, or, nearer to home for most, in the woods and lakes of the area between Georgian Bay and the Ottawa River.

Here where the *voyageurs* once traded with the Hurons for beaver pelts, Ontarians build their summer cottages and moor their boats. Particularly lovely are Lakes Muskoka, Rosseau and Joseph. Reminders of the Huron-French past in this part of Ontario are preserved in the restored mission of Sainte-Marie-among-the-Hurons

near Midland. In the seventeenth century, Sainte-Marie was the only inland European settlement north of Mexico.

Not all the province's citizens relax in cottage country. Some prefer to stow tent and supplies in a canoe and follow the paddles of the *voyageurs* along the old canoe routes that wind through Algonquin Provincial Park.

Algonquin is vast enough to enable the hermit in all of us to find peace and seclusion. It is a unique world of sun-dappled lakes, verdant forests, bright stars, sheltering rocks, squishy bogs and soft, pebbled shores made for daydreaming. Mornings by a lake in Algonquin are the stuff that trusted old memories are made of. Filmy mists lift from the still waters as the sun begins its new ascent, the strange mad call of the loon is the only sound to be heard, and the time-worn pines crest the land as far as the eye can see. In the evening when the moon comes up, if you are lucky you can hear the wolves sing.

Algonquin, and Killarney Provincial Park farther north, were the inspiration for the artists of the Group of

ONTARIO

Seven. Spurning British artistic traditions hitherto common in Canada, the Group's seven painters – A.Y. Jackson, J.E.H. MacDonald, Fred Varley, Arthur Lismer, Lawren Harris, Franklin Carmichael and A.J. Casson – looked to the wilderness beauty of Algonquin and Ontario's north for the inspiration for their rugged, bold, individualistic canvases. Their work, along with that of their colleague, Tom Thomson, who drowned mysteriously in an Algonquin lake, has achieved international acclaim. (Many of these distinctly Canadian masterpieces, painted mostly during the 1920s and 1930s, are on

Whether in summer right and center right, or in winter above, the Niagara Falls – where the vast river, divided by the international boundary, plunges over the escarpment into a deep gorge – is one of the most exciting sights in the world. Tours by bus, cable-rail cars and the "Whirlpool Aerocar" this page show the Niagara River and the aptly named Horseshoe Falls facing page and overleaf to their best advantage. The curving crest of Horseshoe Falls extends around 3,000 feet, over which the river drops a thundering 162 feet.

display at the McMichael Canadian Collection at Kleinburg, within easy driving distance from Toronto.)

The further north you go in Ontario the more you are nonplussed by the enormity of the province. Even northern cities like Sault Ste. Marie on the waterway between Lakes Huron and Superior, and Thunder Bay on the northwest shore of Lake Superior, seem dwarfed by the immensity of the surrounding landscape, yet the former has a population of over 81,000 and is an important lumber and steel center, while Thunder Bay, with close to 110,000 citizens, is the terminus of the St. Lawrence Seaway. Much of the prairie grain finds its way to the

"Lakehead", as Thunder Bay is known, whence it begins its long journey through the Great Lakes to distant markets abroad.

The north is Canadian Shield country, a land of sheer cliffs, dense forests, white-water rivers, countless lakes, and giant outcrops of rock billions of years old. It is accessible to the visitor through spectacular wilderness parks like Quetico, Lake Superior, Ouimet Canyon, and Rainbow Falls. It is a land suited to the hardy and resourceful, and that is what Northerners are.

In addition to lumber, northern Ontario is mining country, courtesy of the shield. Kirkland Lake, Timmins,

Sudbury, Spar Island, Cobalt, Kidd Creek, and Manitou-wadge Lake are all northern mining communities. Their output of zinc, silver, gold, copper, cobalt and other minerals helps keep Ontario prosperous.

Every July 1, when Canada celebrates its birthday, Ontario does, too. On the occasion of its centennial celebration back in 1967, the birthday song of the year was "Ontario – A place to stand and a place to grow". For Ontarians, despite the uncertainties that plague all industrial societies in the late twentieth century, their enormous province is still as rich in possibilities and promise as it ever was.

QUEBEC

As the Rhine and Danube are to Europe, so the St. Lawrence is to Canada, in particular, to the province of Quebec. For it was on the banks of this majestic river that *les Canadiens* laid the foundations for the Canadian nation. In the process, they created in their home province of Quebec, a unique, vibrant culture that has endured for centuries to the enrichment of all Canada.

Ever since that distant July day in 1534 when the French explorer Jacques Cartier sailed across the Gulf of St. Lawrence, planted a crude cross on the high cliffs of Gaspé, claiming the land for France, and then continued up the St. Lawrence River, *Saint-Laurent,* as the river is known to Quebeckers, has always been a leading player in the saga of Canada's development.

Fortunes in furs were traded on the St. Lawrence; French, English, and Indians fought for control of the river; and for explorers it was the highway into the unknown interior.

Originally, though, the lands of the St. Lawrence and furs which the Indians were willing to trade with th French.

Over the next sixty years French involvement i Canada was limited to a fur-trading post established Tadoussac, just east of Quebec City.

In the end, private curiosity rather than official polic was to bring Quebec – and Canada – into being. Samuel d Champlain, soldier, explorer and geographer, had fir sighted Canada in 1603. Two years later, he had bee present at the founding of Port Royal in Nova Scotia. O July 2, 1608, the thirty-eight-year-old Champlain returne to the St. Lawrence as part of a trading expedition of Pier du Gua, Sieur de Monts.

Selecting a natural rock citadel near the India village of Stadacona and overlooking the St. Lawrenc River, Champlain built a two-storey wooden *habitatio* The Indians called the site Quebec, meaning "where th river narrows," and so did Champlain.

Champlain soon found himself embroiled in th

Greater Montreal is the second largest French-speaking metropolis in the world. It has over 550 churches and, ironically, more bars than almost any other North American city! Situated on an island, the city is connected to the mainland by eleven vehicular bridges, five railway bridges and one tunnel. The ultra-modern metro facing page top left h silent rubber-tired trains, while equally modern are th Royal Bank building left and the superb shopping are Complex Desjardin facing page below and top right. Quebec's eccentric Théâtre Midi is pictured above.

the river itself were something of a disappointment. Cartier had come in search of diamonds and gold and a route to China and India. This northern land thwarted him on both counts. He found no gold, and the westward route to Asia that the St. Lawrence seemed to promise proved to be a dead end, for Cartier found his way west along the river blocked by the Lachine Rapids, near Montreal. The only thing that saved Canada, as Cartier called this new land, mistaking the Indian word for village, "kanata," for the name of the country, was its abundance of luxurious

tribal wars between the Algonquins and the Iroquo Siding with the Algonquins, the chief suppliers of furs the French, Champlain used his European weapons help them. Although they retreated before Champlai muskets, the Iroquois were certainly not defeated. And the small colony of New France slowly expanded alon the St. Lawrence, the Iroquois were to extract vengean many times.

The first settlers to come to Quebec, Louis Hébert, apothecary from Paris, Madame Hébert, and their thre children, arrived in 1617. Other families soon followe Europe's great Counter Reformation movement broug

priests flocking to New France, eager to win Indian converts to Catholicism. Settlers and clergy alike tilled the land, but it was hard to keep men at the slow, tedious business of farming when escape and a life of adventure as a *coureur de bois* beckoned in the great fur-rich hinterland. With the result that at the time of Champlain's death on Christmas Day, 1635, furs, not farms, dominated New France, whose population numbered less than 300 permanent European residents.

However, the struggling little communities at Quebec, Montreal, and Trois Rivières soon began to grow in a more regular fashion due to the energies of Françoise de Laval. Bishop Laval's arrival in Quebec in 1659 marked the beginning of the Roman Catholic Church's ascend-

Mont Royal, a former volcano which is now the site of the Parc du Mont Royal, affords magnificent views of the city of Montreal below, left, and facing page top. The glittering *night-time view of the city facing page below was photographed from the 45th floor of the Canadian Imperial Bank of Commerce Building.*

QUEBEC

Quebec is the only walled North American city north of Mexico. Although it was actually founded in 1608 by Samuel de Champlain, Jacques Cartier originally discovered the site and attempted to set up a colony there over half a century earlier. Inside the walls of the city is the Citadel, perched on the summit of Cap Diamant which rises 350 feet above the St. Lawrence River. The fortress is now the headquarters of the famous Royal 22nd Regiment, and during the summer months the Changing of the Guard there is well worth seeing. Along the edge of the cliff is the Promenade des Gouverneurs which descends, by means of several terraces, from the Plains of Abraham to Dufferin Terrace, and affords the visitor several spectacular views. Looking away from the river, one can see the world-famous hotel, the Château Frontenac below, which dominates the Place d'Armes. Outside the walls are the Government Buildings right and facing page top, where the National Assembly meets. The buildings, which were constructed in renaissance style, date from 1886.

ancy to a position of power equal to that of Quebec's secular authorities, a position it was to hold for the next three centuries.

But neither church nor colony could prosper as long as the lightning raids of the fierce Iroquois, now the allies of the English colonists to the south, went unchecked. At Laval's instigation, King Louis XIV dispatched the Carignan-Salières regiment to New France and the bloody skirmishes with the Iroquois were brought under control. Relative peace and the arrival, in 1665, of Jean Talon as the king's civil representative, or *intendant*, provided the final impetus needed to solidify settlement in the colony. To encourage settlement, Talon offered large grants of land or *seigneuries* to officers of the Carignan-Salières regiment. Free passage and the promise of land also encouraged many peasants to leave France. These settlers or *habitants* were provided with land in a *seigneury*. These narrow-fronted, deep, individual land lots, *rangs* stretching back from the banks of the St. Lawrence, and later the Richelieu and Ottawa rivers, can be seen to this day.

The Church was a source of strength and creativity in New France. Religious orders of nuns, in particular the Ursulines, established hospitals, missions, and schools.

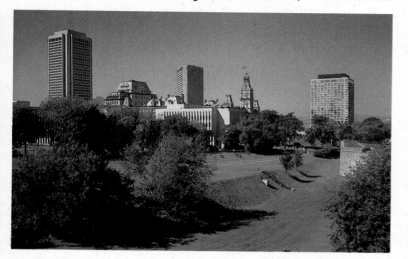

Every community had its own church, and to ensure that these buildings redounded to the greater glory of God and served as an inspiration for His flock, Bishop Laval founded the *École des Arts et Métiers* at present-day Beaupré. Here was born the great tradition of French Canadian painting and woodcarving which makes Quebec's edifices, both religious and secular, so distinct.

Although the population of New France grew from a little over 3,000 in 1666 to 65,000 a century later, the colony could not match the ever-increasing British presence in North America; some one million strong by the mid-eighteenth century.

Montreal was first visited by Jacques Cartier in 1535 when it was still an Indian village called Hochelag. In 1642 Paul de Chomedey, Sieur de Maisonneuve, established the first settlement there, called Ville-Marie, and today Montreal is a thriving city, and the largest inland seaport in the world. It has a rich and varied cultural tradition, and the Place des Arts is the home of the renowned Montreal Symphony Orchestra. A view of Dorchester Street, looking east facing page bottom, shows St. James Cathedral, the Queen Elizabeth Hotel, the Sun Life Building and the Place Ville-Marie. Pictured below is the green-domed St. Joseph Oratoire.

QUEBEC

In Europe wars between France and England fuelled the tensions that already existed between their colonies as a result of the ceaseless quest for furs. The establishment of the Hudson's Bay Company by the English in 1670 only spurred New France's adventurous explorers to travel further afield in the service of the *fleur-de-lis*. In 1673 Louis Joliet and the Jesuit, Jacques Marquette, canoed down the Mississippi as far as the Arkansas River. Nine years later René-Robert Cavelier, Sieur de La Salle, followed Joliet all the way to the Gulf of Mexico, naming the enormous territory he passed through Louisiana, in honor of the king. And Pierre Gaultier de Varennes, Sieur de La Vérendrye, of Trois Rivières, and his sons explored the great plains from Saskatchewan to the Dakotas. But although La Vérendrye built forts as he went and Pierre Le Moyne, Sieur d'Iberville repeatedly harassed the English at Hudson Bay, the young colony, so enormous on paper, was impossible to defend.

The outbreak of the Seven Years' War in 1756 was the harbinger of New France's fall. Louisbourg, the supposedly impregnable French fortress on Cape Breton Island, fell in 1758; Fort Duquesne, today's Pittsburgh, fell the following autumn, and in 1759 General James Wolfe laid siege to the walled city of Quebec. In the ensuing battle, Wolfe was mortally wounded, but he died knowing victory was his. His opponent, the Marquis de Montcalm, hampered always by France's indifference to the war in North America and the ineptitude of his superior, Governor Vaudreuil, expired the following day with the bitter knowledge that New France was lost.

In September of 1760, Governor Vaudreuil surrendered the colony, and by the terms of the Treaty of Paris signed in 1763, all the French lands of the St. Lawrence and beyond passed to the British crown.

But if the unique homogeneous society of New

Montreal facing page *stands at the heart of the St. Lawrence River, on an island which is 30 miles long and 9 miles wide. It is dominated by Mont Royal, 750 feet high, from where the photograph facing page below was taken. The city hums with activity, and a wander through the business areas and the port serves to confirm that this city is well and truly alive! The city is headquarters for four of Canada's great chartered banks, as well as insurance and financial organizations and the Montreal Stock Exchange.*

Quebec City right and above right *is a metropolis steeped in history, and wherever you go you will find monuments and ancient churches and other structures dating from the seventeenth and eighteenth centuries.* Overleaf *The Château Frontenac towers over Quebec City.*

QUEBEC

Capital of the province of Quebec, Quebec City these pages is unique in every way. It is a natural citadel standing where the St. Lawrence River first narrows. It is almost entirely French-speaking, and is, first and foremost, an administrative and cultural center. One of its most famous landmarks is the Château Frontenac below left and facing page. Quebec is the largest of Canada's provinces occupying an area of 594,860-square-miles. The waters of Hudson Bay extend down its western coast to James Bay and its southern coastline is washed by the Gulf of St. Lawrence. Quebec City itself, successfully combining ancient and modern, boasts an exquisite old town as well as several fine examples of contemporary architecture including La Concorde Hotel left. The turrets of the beautifully preserved Manège Militaire below gleam in the sunlight.

France had lacked the numbers to withstand the military onslaught of the English, it certainly possessed the inner spirit and cohesion to not only endure but in time prosper, keeping alive to this day the French fact in the English-speaking world of North America.

Oddly enough, in the first years following the fall of New France, this task was not too difficult. The British, anxious over the rumblings of discontent in their American colonies, had no desire to add to their troubles by provoking their new French subjects. French civil law and seigneurial customs were not tampered with, and far

QUEBEC

from decrying the Roman Catholic Church's influence in the province, successive British governors welcomed its stabilizing conservative force.

In this climate *les Canadiens* were not willing to join with the American revolutionaries, who promised them liberty but could not guarantee the preservation of French customs and language.

The arrival of Loyalists in Quebec, and later of traders and merchants from New England, convinced the French of the rightness of their position. English and American mercantile interests rapidly came to dominate Quebec's cities and the newcomers were not slow to express their dislike of Quebec's traditional ways.

By 1791, the number of Loyalists settled around the Great Lakes warranted the division of old Quebec into Upper Canada (Ontario) and Lower Canada (Quebec). With their original territories diminished and their economy in English hands, the French turned their gaze inward, adhering to the culture and values which had served them well in pre-conquest days.

As money and progress spoke for the English, the Catholic clergy and tradition were the voice of the French. Quebec took refuge in the seigneurial farm where,

encouraged by the Church, her sons and daughters raised their large families and clung tenaciously to all things French. In the province's church-run schools and colleges, French language and culture, not commerce, were the subjects of instruction, for the desired result was to be a class of priests, notaries, and doctors, not entrepreneurs, merchants, and industrialists.

The French retreat, however, was an uneasy one. In the end, poverty, overcrowding, successive poor crops, and government indifference to their needs turned the *habitants* into embittered *Patriotes*, ripe for rebellion. Insurrection came in 1837 and 1838, with the rebels' proud cry: *"Avant tout je suis Canadien!"* ("Before all else I am a Canadian!") defying the English, whose loyalties often lay across the sea or across the border. The rebellion was ruthlessly repressed. Twelve of the leaders were hanged and about sixty others shipped to the penal colonies in Australia.

The momentum gained by the insurrection was not to be lost, however, and thanks to the brilliant political

Quebec City these pages has an old world charm seen in few other North American cities or towns. Many of the narrow streets in the Old Town are lined with little houses of warm, pink-gray stone, splashes of color provided by brightly painted house fronts below and bottom. Above the streets of the Old Town towers the magnificent Château Frontenac seen facing page left behind the Furniture Museum, and facing page below right. One of the city famous restaurants, "Aux Anciens Canadiens," is pictured below left with the Government Buildings towering behind it.

trategies of men like Sir Georges-Étienne Cartier, thirty ears later the way was paved for Quebec's participation vith Ontario, New Brunswick, and Nova Scotia in the ounding of the Canadian national state. Canadian Confederation came into being on July 1, 1867. On ntering Confederation, Quebec took as her motto the hrase *Je me souviens* (I remember). And even now, almost 20 years after the modern province of Quebec came into eing, the pull of the past is strong here, far stronger than 1 any other part of Canada.

Not surprisingly, the glory that was New France lives n in Quebec City, where the province's history began. ucked behind the city's ancient stone walls, Quebec's arrow, winding streets divide rows of steep, gabled ouses, looking much as they did when Wolfe's army ntered the city so long ago. The tomb of Montcalm is oused in the venerable old Ursuline Convent. Founded in 642 by Madame de La Peltrie and Mother Marie de Incarnation, the convent is Canada's oldest nunnery and ducational institute for women.

Rising above Quebec City's old houses and shuttered shop-fronts are the spires of her numerous churches, the noblest of which is perhaps the Basilica of Notre-Dame. For three centuries the faithful have prayed to the Madonna in this splendid cathedral, the culmination of the artistry of the famed Baillargé family.

The *Hôtel-Dieu* Hospital and Bishop Laval's *Séminaire de Québec* are further reminders of the dominance of the Catholic Church in the life of Quebec. As in Ireland, Catholicism was Quebec's sustaining force and the rallying point of a people governed by outsiders.

In the 1960s, however, young *Québécois* began to look critically at their world, questioning whether their religious-based society, strong on humanism and weak on commerce, was not the main reason for their inferior economic status within their own province. Thus was born the Quiet Revolution, which saw reforms in education, politics and business designed to make Quebeckers *maîtres chez nous* (masters in our own house).

In the capital, Quebec City, the struggles of old are not forgotten but the challenge of the present – and the future – is met head-on in the National Assembly. With

QUEBEC

Visitors come from all over the world to see Quebec's glorious autumn colors these pages. Artists and photographers try to capture what they see in paint or on film, while others come simply to absorb...The most famous region is the Laurentian Range, which runs parallel to the St. Lawrence River, just north of Montreal and Quebec City. A wide variety of recreational activities is available here, including excellent skiing facilities in winter. La Maurice National Park, which was established in 1970, is a heavily wooded and largely unspoiled section of the Laurentian Mountains. Situated at Grand' Mère and Shawinigan, the park is almost equidistant from Montreal and Quebec. It has numerous beautiful lakes, a wide choice of hiking trails and several well-equipped camping sites.

statues of Wolfe and Montcalm guarding the entrance, the Assembly echoes to some of the liveliest debates heard in Canada in many years: Should Quebec separate from the rest of Canada? Should Quebec be a bilingual or unilingual province? How can Quebec gain control over its economic destiny?

Most Quebeckers do not favor separation, fearing, as their forebears did, that to stand alone without the rest of Canada would mean sure absorption into the United States. Instead, they see the need to strengthen their society through the use of their language, not only in the home, the school, and the Church, but by making it the working tongue of business, science, and technology.

Nowhere is this feeling more apparent than in Montreal. More than forty-five percent of Quebeckers reside in Montreal, the largest French-speaking city after Paris. Spread across the two large islands of Montréal and Jésus and the two smaller islands of Perrot and Bizard, and surrounded by the St. Lawrence, Montreal's fortunes were founded on the fur trade and her admirable position as a trading center. Confederation and the great railway boom of nineteenth-century Canada solidified Montreal's position as Canada's pre-eminent commercial center, but the men who wheeled and dealed on St. James Street were all English speakers. Nothing better tells the tale of English dominance of Quebec's economy than the name of this street, the heart of Montreal's financial district – until the Quiet Revolution nobody ever dreamed of calling St. James Street *Rue St-Jacques*.

Canada's railways, banks, insurance companies and giant corporations of all kinds traditionally had their head offices in Montreal, where their employees spoke English if they wished to make it to the top.

The strong nationalist sentiment abroad in Quebec, epitomized by the *Parti Québécois*, is a result of these limited opportunities and has led to the adoption of French as the working language of all Quebec.

If Quebeckers have second thoughts about leaving Canada, their fellow Canadians certainly do not wish to see them go. Apart from the bonds of shared history, the verve and vitality, sparkle, *joie de vivre*, and the overwhelming cultural security of Quebec fascinate English-speaking Canada.

Whether in the dimly lit restaurants of old Quebec City where conversation over fine French cuisine ranges from the political doings in French-speaking Africa to the latest plays in Paris, and the new novels of Quebec authors; or in Montreal's smoky *boîtes à chanson* where the students from McGill and Concordia and the *Université de Québec* gather till the early hours of the morning to drink wine, argue over the province's future, and lustily sing the songs of old and new Quebec, Quebeckers display none of that crisis of identity that often bedevils other Canadians.

Montreal itself is a city of many moods. Her elegant shopping complexes and gleaming glass towers zing with that restless energy so peculiarly North American, yet

The coastline of the Gaspé Peninsula these pages, which cuts eastwards into the Gulf of St. Lawrence, has to be seen to be believed. Take the road from Ste. Anne des Monts to Rivière au Renard and the Florillon National Park, *through the Gaspé and along the coast to Percé, and you will find countless tiny fishing villages nestling at the foot of menacing cliffs.*

Overleaf St. Joachim-de-Tourelle.

they seem to defer to rather than overwhelm the older treasures of *vieux Montréal* – the Notre-Dame Church with its vaulted starry dome; the beautiful marble and ivory high altar in the cathedral of Mary, Queen of the World; the fieldstone *Château de Ramezay*, which was the early eighteenth-century seat of government in French Canada; and the old fur warehouses of the *Place d'Youville*.

Nowhere in Canada are the arts more lively than in Montreal. Poets, painters, singers, musicians, playwrights and film-makers celebrate the vitality of Quebec's culture. But in the arts "French only" is not the rule. Montreal has the largest Jewish population in Canada, and its influence, like that of the Italians, Vietnamese, Africans, Haitians, Portuguese, Greeks, Hungarians, Poles, Czechs and the English, is very much felt in the cosmopolitanism that makes Montreal such an exciting place to live.

Montreal is probably the best known of Canada's cities. The world remembers the 1976 Olympic Games, and Expo' 67 nine years earlier. Incidentally, "Expo" lives on in the fascinating pavilions of Man and His World, which are still visited by thousands of tourists every year. But if

QUEBEC

The village of Percé this page and overleaf clings to the very tip of the Gaspé Peninsula. Lying 46 miles from the community of Gaspé, the village is named after the world famous rock, the Roche Percé, which dominates its beach. This strange natural phenomenom is the result of a geological upheaval which took place millions of years ago, and it was behind the rock that Cartier first anchored his three ships in July 1534. Percé is a popular resort, offering panoramic terraces, nature trails, excursions around the capes, fishing – and excellent fish restaurants – arts and crafts centers, and a wide choice of hotel and other lodging places.

you were to ask Montrealers what they think their city is famous for, the instant response would be *"Les Canadiens!"*

When the Montreal Canadiens hockey team takes to the ice in the Montreal Forum, a full house of wildly enthusiastic fans follows every scrape of the blade and slap of the puck. Almost every small boy dreams of wearing the Canadiens' famous red sweater, and winter finds them all practising furiously on rinks and countless frozen ponds throughout the province.

Although less than twenty percent of Quebeckers live on the land, rural Quebec still exerts a considerable hold on the province's consciousness. Anyone seeking to understand this complex province should spend time exploring the countryside. Only one-tenth of Quebec's vast lands are suitable for agriculture and much of the arrable land is found in the Eastern Townships, along the shores of the St. Lawrence, and in the terraces and tablelands that shelter behind the Gaspé Peninsula. It is Quebeckers in these places that keep alive the heritage of the *habitants*. Where first the Indians hunted and trapped, the *habitants* built their stone houses with the big, warm kitchens where even today visitors and children returning home from the city love to gather to sing, play cards, and talk the night away.

If young, urban Quebeckers are strong nationalists, their country relatives share this sentiment. *Joual*, the language of old Quebec, is spoken widely among rural Quebeckers, who find its eccentricities and odd expressions further proof of their province's unique culture.

In picturesque **St. Lawrence** communities like La Pocatière, Saint-Denis, **and Kamouraska** (site of Anne Hébert's smoldering **novel of passion** and cruelty), the Church is still a vibrant **force, perhaps** almost as much for social reasons as for **spiritual ones.** Quebeckers are gregarious people, generous, **sentimental** and fond of each other's company. With the soul refreshed at mass parishioners are likely to gather for a convivial pot luck Sunday meal at the parish church.

Tourtière, chopped veal or pork pie; *six-pâtes*, deep pot-pie made out of partridge, quail, hare, potatoes and bacon, all flavored with cloves; *ragoût de boulettes et de pattes de cochon*, meat-balls and pig's feet stew; and *habitant* pea soup made with white peas, are traditional recipes known to every cook, although it must be said that

QUEBEC

Lying on opposite sides of the Gaspé Peninsula are Rivière-la-Madelaine below which looks across the St. Lawrence estuary towards northern Quebec, and Port Daniel right, lying on the Baie des Chaleurs. The beautiful photograph facing page top shows a sunset over the St. Lawrence River, while Capuchins facing page below wakes up to a calm summer day. The principal town on the Peninsula is Gaspé itself, which today has a population of around 18,000. Now a bustling commercial and industrial center, it was here, some 450 years ago, that Cartier first took possession of Canada in the name of the King of France. To commemorate the fourth centenary of this event, the people of Gaspé held a festival during which a cross was erected in memory of the wooden cross which Cartier had planted there back in 1534. The name Gaspé derives from "Gespeg," an Indian word meaning "end."

patates frites, the french fries or chips that English speaking Canadians gobble up, are also great favorites in Quebec. Wine imported from France is readily available and is considered a necessary adjunct to the enjoyment of most meals.

As the deep blue St. Lawrence flows on to its meeting with the Atlantic Ocean, it passes little fishing hamlets where rows of cod are set to dry on wooden platforms under sunny summer skies. This is the Gaspé region where the rivers teem with salmon, the cliffs are high and steep, the beaches quiet and secluded, the crab marvellously delicious, and the people friendly and outgoing.

Gaspé is a must for photographers, painters, and poets with an eye for the stern beauty of nature's mature face. And, of course, Percé Rock, probably Quebec's most famous landmark, still stands aloof in the indigo waters of the gulf. When Champlain first saw Percé, the old rock had four arches. By 1845 only one remained, which may still be seen and, at low tide, examined.

Once upon a time, the sea must have been higher than it is today, for the smooth surface of Percé's top has obviously been planed clean by the waves of countless centuries. What the future will do to Percé is anyone's guess.

While no one can foretell the future, Quebeckers have reason to be optimistic about their province. Quebec's enormous northland is the source of great riches in lumber, minerals and hydro electric power. Quebec's culture has never been healthier and has taken its rightful place in the world-wide community of French-speaking nations. And, at home in Quebec, at long last, industry and commerce speak in French.

Almost everyone occasionally yearns to get away from it all – to drift along on some wide, smooth-flowing river, sunlight glinting on the water and dappling the green, wooded banks. No sound but water lapping and trees rustling. In Canada, fulfilling this fantasy is just as far away as beautiful New Brunswick. With its backdoor on Quebec and the State of Maine, and all the Atlantic provinces before it, New Brunswick is 27,985 square miles of rivers, forests, farms and beaches. With its small population of a little over 700,000, there is space a-plenty for urban runaways.

With almost eighty-eight percent of New Brunswick's land covered with forests, finding a leafy refuge should present no problem. As for rivers, as a map of New Brunswick will show, the province is laced with them: The Saint John, Miramichi, Restigouche, Madawaska, Petitcodiac, Kennebecasis, Kouchibouguac, Tantramar, Canaan…If you set off to follow the course of one of these rivers, you will find yourself slowly becoming part of its unique life and character. Choosing the river for your getaway is the only hard decision you will have to make.

To many New Brunswickers (in particular, those born within sight or sound of it), the Saint John is the fairest river of all. Certainly, its route does offer scenery as varied as the form of the river itself. Starting in the high forests of northern Maine, the Saint John crosses into Canada and winds its slender way through the thick Acadian forests of New Brunswick's northwestern Madawaska County, so named for the Madawaska River that flows into the Saint John near the thriving pulp-producing town of Edmunston. When about seventy percent of a forest's trees

are soft woods – spruce and fir – and the remaining thirty percent hardwoods – birch and maple – it is classified as an Acadian forest.

Madawaska County had always been a lumber region. During the nineteenth century, its forests resounded with the blows of countless axes as tree after tree was felled to build men-of-war for the British navy and merchant ships for traders determined to exploit the riches of a fast shrinking world.

Lumber made the fortunes of some men, and the reputations of others. For men like "Main John" Glasier it did both. A gaunt, craggy giant of a man who, so legend

Situated in New Brunswick's Saint John River Region, Kings Landing Historical Settlement these pages is a fascinating restoration of village life in the central Saint John River Valley between the years of 1790 and 1870. The Saint John River, originally named "Oa-lus-tuk" or "goodly river," has its source in the northern forest region in the State of Maine and meanders all the way to the Bay of Fundy. Illustrated here are: above the picturesque Kings Head Inn, facing page weatherboarded Perley House, and top and left Joslin Farm, in front of which stands a young girl in historical costume, ready to answer any visitors' questions.

NEW BRUNSWICK

has it, was never seen by friend or foe – or Mrs. Glasier, for that matter – without his tall black hat, he was a pioneer lumberman in the Madawaska. He earned his nickname from a raid he led into neighboring Maine in order to smash a competitor's dam which was impeding the flow of the Saint John River. In those days, lumberjacks used to pull the felled timber by oxen teams to the banks of the Saint John, where it was lashed into rafts and floated downriver to the saw mills as soon as the river's covering of winter ice broke up. With the Saint John not flowing at full capacity, Glasier's logs could not clear the Grand Falls,

a turbulent gorge situated south of Edmunston, and as a result, were speedily, and unprofitably, pulped.

"Main John" accomplished his mission in Maine. With his logs continuing to clear the Grand Falls, Glasier went on to become a member of New Brunswick's legislature. His nickname lives on today in lumber camps all over North America where the boss is referred to as the "main john."

Squabbles between New Brunswick and Maine over timber cutting rights in the Upper Saint John River valley were quite common during the nineteenth century, and lumbermen on both sides of the border frequently took to each other with their peavies (short poles with iron hooks used for moving logs). Becoming tired of the diplomatic delays involved in settling one such dispute, the "Pork and Beans War" of 1837, Madawaskans resolved the matter to their own satisfaction by simply declaring themselves to be citizens of the République du Madawaska. The mythical republic lives on, albeit as a droll local joke, and its handsome flag of a proud bald eagle and six red stars flutters rakishly over Edmunston, its "capital." The stars

Kings Landing Historical Settlement occupies a 300 acre riverside site. Pictured above and above left is Lint House, whose traditionally costumed resident still practices the crafts of a bygone era. A view of Hageman House can be seen right; and left a saw which is genuinely horse-powered. The importance of preserving

Canada's history makes this living museum a truly worthwhile enterprise. Transported back in time, the visitor can even eat at the Kings Head Inn, which features a menu of foods which would have been served in the 1800's. Overleaf New Brunswick Cemetery glows mysteriously in evening light.

NEW BRUNSWICK

represent the six dominant peoples of Madawaska – Acadians, Indians, French, English, Irish, and Americans. This vibrant mix contributes much to the lively spirit that surfaces not only in the conversation of Madawaskans, but also in the old music, songs and dances still executed with such verve in these parts. French is the mother tongue of Madawaskans, but like most of New Brunswick, they are at ease in both of Canada's official languages, as well as the republic's own dialect, *brayon*.

Up until it reaches Grand Falls, the Saint John is a rather subdued river, seeming to be almost intimidated by the forests that arch above it. At the Grand Falls, it suddenly finds its own voice, and plunges with noisy, spray-tossed fury into the gorge 150 feet below. Although this mighty surge of water has been harnessed to supply power for the Grand Falls hydro electric power station,

one of the largest power plants in the Maritimes, it has lost none of that dramatic force that Main John Glasier took up arms to defend over a century ago.

Seemingly satisfied with its exertions at the falls, the river settles down and slowly widens as it passes through the type of countryside Beethoven must have had in mind when he composed the *Pastoral Symphony*. Now you are in a land of tidy farms whose gentle meadows come down to meet the reeds and wavy grasses at the river's bank.

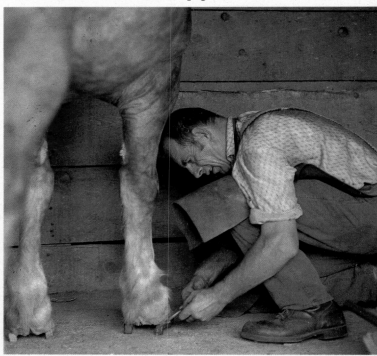

New Brunswick is one of the Atlantic Provinces, along with Newfoundland, Nova Scotia and Prince Edward Island. Situated in the extreme east of Canada, these provinces all have important lumbering overleaf and fishing industries, while a major specialist farming crop is potatoes. The ports of the Atlantic Provinces are very important to Canadian and United States trade, especially when the St. Lawrence freezes in winter.

Many of the crafts which were carried out in the past have been perpetuated here at Kings Landing. The blacksmith can be seen at work right and above right, while in Joslin House, a woman sorts wool before she spins it on the traditional spinning wheel above left. Pictured facing page is Morehouse Farm.

NEW BRUNSWICK

Here are fields of potato plants, blossoming in a profusion of delicate purples and pinks. In the pastures cows and sheep graze contentedly, and frisky colts toss their dappled manes, delighting in the warm sunny skies. Occasionally, a weathered log pier projects into the river, and small boats may be encountered lazily plying its backwater reaches.

Called by the Micmac Indians "Oo-lahs-took," meaning "goodly river," nowhere is the bounty of the Saint John more apparent than in the fertile farming valley that stretches from Drummond, south of Grand Falls, to Woodstock, just west of Fredericton, the province's capital. The valley is peaceful and serene, no matter what the season. But you have to be there in spring to savor a delicacy quite distinct to New Brunswick – fiddleheads. Just after spring runoff, the first fronds of the ostrich fern poke up through the moist earth along the banks of the Saint John. These fronds, or fiddleheads, so called because of their resemblance to the curled head of a violin, require only a few minutes simmering and a little butter to release their subtle flavor.

Much of the produce of the valley, including fiddleheads, is processed and frozen in the town of Florenceville, and eventually makes its way to dinner tables right across North America.

Where the Saint John stretches itself at Hartland, a fine old covered bridge spans the river. Said to be the longest in the world, the bridge is high enough and wide enough to permit the safe passage of a laden hay wagon.

Whether great-grandfather sneaked a kiss from his best girl as they walked over the Hartland covered bridge

The interior of Morehouse Farm, Kings Landing, is illustrated right. Every detail of the room is perfect, from the large open fireplace to the wooden milk churn in the corner. The wholesome country food which constituted the bulk of the diet all those years ago is still cooked to traditional recipes. Perley House, shrouded in mist, can be seen above, while above right Perley Store stocks household provisions which would have been very familiar to housewives in the eighteenth and nineteenth centuries. Beeswax candles, flavorings such as cherry, lemon and vanilla, jars of preserved and pickled fruits and vegetables and a choice of soaps are among the goods lining the shelves, all packaged in old-fashioned jars, tins and boxes. A water-powered sawmill is shown facing page.

NEW BRUNSWICK

A selection of interiors photographed at Kings Landing Historical Settlement these pages are accurate representations of the sort of rooms inhabited by earlier residents of New Brunswick. A friendly formality was the order of the day as far as front parlors were concerned facing page top and bottom, and shutters were often used instead of curtains. Most people were skilled at something, be it knitting right, quilting far right or child-rearing below!
Overleaf A piece of traditional farm equipment can be seen in the foreground of this photograph of Hagerman House. One of the skills used in making such a piece of equipment is that of the wheelwright, who is both carpenter and blacksmith.

on their way home from a gospel meeting or a dance, no one knows, but contrary to popular belief, covered bridges were not built with courting couples in mind. Bridges were covered to preserve them. An uncovered bridge had a life of no more than fifteen years before rot made it unsafe; a covered one was good for at least eighty years.

From hospitable Woodstock to Fredericton the Saint John has undergone a complete transformation, thanks to the building of the Mactaquac Dam and its adjacent hydro electric power development. Actually, at this point the Saint John is no longer a river, it is more like a lake. Whether the river's new face is an improvement or not depends on just whom you're talking to. No issue so inflamed the normally sanguine Saint John River people than the building of the dam in 1967, which necessitated the flooding of so many river communities.

Fredericton, of course, is really never in need of improvement. The gracious charm and tranquillity that

make New Brunswick such a perfect retreat seem somehow caught forever here in Fredericton, the province capital. Situated on the banks of the Saint John, about ninety miles upstream from the Bay of Fundy, Fredericton is considered, with some justification, to be the loveliest city in Canada. Of all the Maritime cities, it best reflect the hearts and minds of those colonial Loyalists who, over two centuries ago, fled north to the region rather than swear allegiance to the new American republic. More than in any other province, the Loyalists have left their stamp on New Brunswick. Here, in a tiny clearing known as Ste. Anne's Point, they laid the foundations of Fredericton, building simple log cabins to house the grand pianos and fine mahogany furniture they brought with them into the wilderness. Thanks to their persistence, this secluded haven on the Saint John River lives on as permanent reminder of the once powerful British presence in North America.

Many of Fredericton's fine public buildings and handsome homes, erected by wealthy lumber men and shipbuilders during the nineteenth century, still line the city's wide elm-shaded streets. The University of New Brunswick, Canada's oldest provincial university, sets the tone for much of Fredericton's rich cultural life. And thanks to the generosity of one of New Brunswick's greatest sons, Lord Beaverbrook, of newspaper fame, the city's Beaverbrook Art Gallery is home to a splendid collection of British and Canadian art. Included in the former are works by Beaverbrook's old friend, Winston Churchill, while the Canadian collection boasts many works by Cornelius Krieghoff, one of the foremost Canadian primitive painters.

Reminders of yesterday are everywhere in Fredericton – Christ Church Cathedral, the old Military Compound, the Legislative Building, and stately Government House, but for a real step back into that bygone Loyalist world, a visit to the Kings Landing Historical Settlement, just west of Fredericton, is a must. Here, the Saint John River still powers the grist mill and the saw mill. Farmers in homespun may be seen tilling the

NEW BRUNSWICK

fields, aided by oxen and a crew of barefoot boys. And women in dimity dresses and lace-trimmed caps knit, sew, cook, churn butter, make candles, blue their laundry, and keep an eye on each other's doings as they did back when the nineteenth century was in its prime.

Leaving Fredericton, the Saint John winds south on the last stages of its long journey toward the city that bears its name. En route, it constantly skirts small islands, placed like so many stepping stones throughout its broad channel. From the woods along the banks the fragrance of lily of the valley is carried on the gentle breeze, and blue

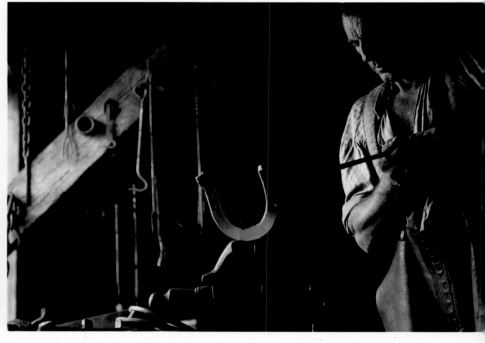

flag iris bloom abundantly as far as the eye can see. All manner of fowl and wildlife inhabit this fertile region, and the streams that flow into the Saint John are alive with plump trout.

The first Loyalists to arrive in New Brunswick settled at the mouth of the Saint John River, in a town named by earlier French colonists in honor of St. John the Baptist. By 1785, the fledgling town had become Canada's first incorporated city. In the days when lumber ruled New

Fred H. Perley's General Merchant Stores above left and facing page below sells nothing but those provisions which would have been available over a century ago. Hand-knitted pullovers of homespun wools, embroidered linen sheets and pillowcases, twine, wax polish, hand- *woven cloth, lace, cotton thread and shoe-stitching thread, and china and glass are among the wide variety of goods available. Ingraham House facing page top has a glorious, well-tended country garden top right and, of course a historically-accurate interior top left.*

NEW BRUNSWICK

Brunswick, the city of Saint John was the hub of the province's commercial activity, a distinction it still retains. With the river, the Bay of Fundy, and a backdrop of green hills, Saint John is a splendidly placed city.

At Lancaster, one of the city's many new suburbs, the river makes a flamboyant exit at the Reversing Falls. At ebb tide, the Saint John drops down a narrow gorge into the Bay of Fundy. When the mighty Fundy tides rise, they reciprocate by sending salt water surging and frothing up the gorge, filling it and flooding over into the upper river itself. So high are these tides that oceangoing super tankers can sail inland when the fall is reversed.

All along New Brunswick's Fundy coast, the antics of Fundy's tides are a never-ending source of fascination. Twice daily, for six hours at a time, they retreat, causing the Bay to "swallow" an extra 3,680,000,000 cubic feet of water, only to advance again, disgorging the same enormous body of water. The prospect of harnessing some of this tidal energy tantalizes New Brunswick. Nova Scotia, just across the Bay, is also intrigued by the idea. Quicksand and mud on the tidal flats pose very real building problems, however. And, although the tides could be harnessed both coming and going, irregularities in their water levels make it likely that there would be times when they would generate too much power, and at others, none at all! Moreover, even if these problems were overcome, the cost of such a project would be enormous. But then so would the amount of electricity generated by the tides.

While Saint John ponders the pros and cons of Fundy power, the city's visitors are also faced with some decision making, although of a much less taxing variety. Should one leave the city for the luxury of the old Atlantic playground along the southwest coast from Saint John, or head off toward the rivers of the east?

No wealthy Canadian or American, circa 1900, would have had any problem picking the right spot – the handsome Algonquin Hotel, at St. Andrews, on the shore of Passamaquoddy Bay. Of course, if you were particularly prosperous, St. Andrews was merely just the jumping off point to your own retreat on one of the nearby Fundy islands. The family of President Franklin Roosevelt, for example, always spent the summer at their thirty-four-room "cottage" on Campobello, now the focal point of the Campobello International Park.

The largest of the Fundy islands, Grand Manan, also has a busy summer season, only its visitors are thousands of nesting birds. Easily accessible by ferry from Black's Harbor, Grand Manan is also a whale watcher's delight, and the perfect spot if you have always fancied living on an island.

But for all those people who will find beachcombing on Grand Manan just the escape they were seeking, some will want to follow the fortunes of just one more river.

The most obvious contrast to the Saint John River is the Miramichi, which flows eastward through the heart of the province to the Gulf of St. Lawrence. Whereas the Saint John flows almost the full length of New Brunswick,

Killeen's Cabin left is just one of 55 buildings that go to make up Kings Landing Historical Settlement. There is a blacksmith shop, a general store, a school, a church, a tavern, an operational sawmill, a working farm and a wide variety of other buildings fulfilling different functions. Cooking to traditional recipes is mainly done over an open fire in cast-iron cookware.

NEW BRUNSWICK

the three short branches of the Miramichi make up an intact river system of no more than 200 miles. The Miramichi owes its beginnings to the retreating glacier of the last Ice Age, and the area through which it flows is so scarred by the glacier's rude departure that it resembles rocky Newfoundland more than the gentle terrain of most of the Saint John's valleys. However, like the Upper Saint John region, this is lumbering country, and tall tales and lusty songs of the old lumber camps are very much part of popular folklore. In fact, rumor has it that that most illustrious son of Miramichi, Lord Beaverbrook, once held up the proceedings at a World War II planning session by insisting that Russia's Joseph Stalin join in on a chorus of "The Jones Boys," an old Miramichi ditty about some lads and their sawmill. Incidentally, this famous news magnate, born Max Aitken in Newcastle, at the mouth of the Miramichi, where his father was the vicar of St. James's Presbyterian Church, took the name "Beaverbrook" from a little stream where he used to fish as a boy.

People might make their living from lumber in the

iramichi, but as every local will tell you, fishing is the eason no one wants to leave the old river, for the liramichi, especially its southwest arm, is stocked with me of the finest Atlantic salmon imaginable.

When Sieur Nicolas Denys was granted the right to l this region by the French government in 1632, he mplained that the noise of the multitude of silvery lmon making their way upstream to spawn was so xcessive that sleep was impossible. While more than ree centuries of solid fishing have made it unlikely that enys' particular kind of insomnia will ever bother nyone who sleeps beside the fast-flowing waters of the liramichi, a day's work with rod and reel usually results in delicious supper.

The Miramichi and the Saint John are New runswick's best known rivers, but as any citizen of Ioncton, that busy French city on the Petitcodiac in the utheast of the province, will tell you, nothing rivals the arkle of their river in spring, the green of her valley in immer, or the vibrancy of her forest colors in fall.

Up north, along the Restigouche, the most famous of salmon rivers, there is a certain amount of polite condescension toward southern rivers, with their open meadows and model farms. Here, where the hills are steep enough to be called mountains, and the forests thick enough to test an experienced woodsman's skills, the powerful Restigouche challenges the most dedicated angler.

And then there are the Nipisiquit, Dungarvon, Kedgwick, Tracadie, and the Gaspereau. In the end, it does not really matter where you wander in New Brunswick, because there is always one more river waiting for you to explore.

Fundy National Park facing page below *is 80 square miles of seaside parkland whose rambling coastline and magnificent forests, streams and tranquil lakes teem with wildlife. Pictured here is Point*

Wolfe covered bridge and dam. The park has a warmed salt-water swimming pool, a natural amphitheater, hiking trails, tennis, golf, fishing and boating, and an arts and crafts school.

The Acadian Coastal Region occupies New Brunswick's "land of plenty," its east coast. The Acadian Historical Village above, top, left and facing page top is a settlement which accurately portrays the Acadian way of life in different parts of New Brunswick from 1780 to 1880. The village has nine farms, whose simplicity in construction and furnishings vividly illustrates the time of austerity which followed the 1755 Expulsion of the Acadians. Here is evidence of a determination to survive by a people deprived of their homes, land and way of life – and evidence of their success!

NOVA SCOTIA

Many Canadian soldiers, sailors, and airmen remember Halifax as their last base prior to departure for the battlefields of Europe during World War II. Halifax, the mainland port nearest the war zone, was the great supply base of a beleaguered Britain. From the fall of France to 1945, her streets swarmed with sailors from all the Allied merchant services. Day and night, her dockyards and ship-fitting plants toiled to repair the casualties of the bloody Battle of the Atlantic, some 7,000 ships in all.

Had these same Canadians visited Halifax back in

December 1917, they would have found a Halifax that was itself one of the bloodiest casualties of that earlier war to end all wars. On December 6th of that year the French steamship *Mont Blanc*, laden with explosives including highly flammable benzol, was making its way into Bedford Basin when it was struck by the Belgian relief ship *Imo*. The impact caused the benzol to ignite.

Shortly after 9:00 a.m., as Halifax settled down to another day's activity, the *Mont Blanc* exploded. Sixteen hundred men, women, and children died in that moment. Thousands were injured and left homeless. The northern part of Halifax was levelled, and hardly a window remained intact throughout the rest of the city. The misery endured by the shocked survivors huddled in make-shift quarters as a fierce winter blizzard swept over the city is movingly recorded by novelist Hugh MacLennan in *Barometer Rising*.

The hazards of war have always been familiar to Haligonians. After all, war, or the promise of it, brought Halifax into being back in 1749. In that year, Colonel Edward Cornwallis, one of King George II's more capable officers, led an expedition of Cockney settlers into Halifax Harbor.

His Majesty's colonies in New England – and, indeed, His Majesty's government – were much perturbed by the presence of French fortifications on nearby Île Royale, that portion of present-day Nova Scotia now known as Cape Breton. Prudence dictated that the English check-mate the French by establishing a similar fortification – Halifax, named for George Dunk, Earl of Halifax.

Situated on a peninsula with tidewater on three sides,

Halifax was to be mistress of a splendid deep-water, ice-free harbor, and custodian of a sheltered inner harbor (Bedford Basin) large enough and deep enough to hold the naval might of all the world's nations. Certainly, a more perfect site for a town destined to be both a citadel of defence and a center of trade could not be imagined.

Unfortunately, imagination was about all Cornwallis had to work with during the town's first years. Typhoid fever, rum, occasional attacks from the indigenous Micmac Indians, and the settlers' indolence often put the town's very survival in doubt. Still, in that first year, work on one of Halifax's great landmarks, St. Paul's Anglican Church, got under way. Completed in 1750, the church has been holding services ever since.

Also in 1750, the good ship *Alderney* brought 353 new settlers to lay the foundation of Dartmouth, across the harbor from Halifax. Two years later, in 1752, the ferry service between Dartmouth and Halifax was established and continues to link the twin cities to this day.

Today, Colonel Cornwallis' garrison is a handsome city of almost 120,000 people and bears the responsibility of being the financial and commercial center of Atlantic Canada with aplomb. And Dartmouth, for years overshadowed by its bigger sister across the harbor, is a prosperous industrial center, with a population nudging 70,000.

But Halifax is still a services town. Much of the twin cities' workforce is employed by Canadian Forces Base Halifax. Ships still ride at anchor in the old Naval Dockyard started by Captain James Cook in 1759. Her Majesty's Canadian Dockyard, as it is called now, is head-

Beautiful Nova Scotia these pages is, along with New Brunswick, Prince Edward Island and Newfoundland, one of Canada's Maritime Provinces. Primarily made up of fertile uplands and valleys, the province is also blessed with great mineral wealth. It is particularly rich in coal, much of which is used in the production of steel.
The sun sets and a pinprick of light can be seen left as Enragee Point Lighthouse warns navigators of treacherous rocks. At Broad Cove facing page right low tide exposes seaweed and pebbles; while facing page left is a view taken at the historical village of Sherbrooke. Goldenrod and summer skies frame a tranquil view of Poirierville on the Isle Madame below.

NOVA SCOTIA

quarters for Maritime Command, the naval arm of Canada's defence forces. And as long as the fleet is in, Halifax will always pulse with that undercurrent of excitement not found in landlocked cities.

The Port of Halifax is world renowned for its modern containerization facilities. Over two million tons of containerized cargo from all over the world are handled annually at the sprawling port complex. Haligonians take the trappings of the port – giant container ships, 45-ton gantry cranes that can move a container every forty-five seconds, and the lift trucks scurrying to and fro – in their stride. After all, as any schoolchild here will tell you, ships of the world have always called at Halifax, and not too many years ago, many of them were Nova Scotia built.

The mid-nineteenth century was good to Halifax, indeed, to all Nova Scotia. The Crimean War, the Indian Mutiny, and the gold rushes in California and Australia all

necessitated the moving of large numbers of people and supplies over vast distances.

Before the age of the airplane, travel meant ships, and ships meant timber. Nova Scotia had timber to spare for shipbuilding. And her sons were eager for the life before the mast. In no time, the docks of Halifax along Water Street became a veritable jam of sailing ships, roistering sailors, and strange and wonderful cargoes. Nova Scotian sailors were known as "Bluenoses," though no one quite knows why.

As the Bluenose fleet grew and grew, finally numbering 3,000 sailing vessels, communities outside Halifax also prospered. Yarmouth, in the southwest of the province, enjoyed great prosperity as the shipbuilding center of Nova Scotia.

Small villages also benefited from the boom, as men in every inlet along the coast got together to build boats. "Built up some Nova Scotia creek!," a favorite sailor's expletive of the day, tells just how completely Nova Scotia gave itself over to the age of sail. The more somber side of this story may be seen in an architectural feature common to Nova Scotian seamen's homes of the period: the widow's walk, whence many a Nova Scotian woman kept lonely vigil, often in vain, for the return of her man.

Halifax, situated right on the Atlantic coast, is Nova Scotia's capital and the largest city of the Atlantic Provinces. The city's Metro Centre and tower blocks provide a somewhat incongruous backdrop to the lovely old town clock which dates from 1803 below left. The white weatherboarded church in Sherbrooke Village can be seen below while the wistful statue of Evangeline is pictured in the foreground of

the Grand Pré Chapel bottom. The small community of Grand Pré, near Wolfville, was a major Acadian settlement in the seventeenth and eighteenth centuries. Brightly painted boats appear to balance on their own reflections in the still waters of Digby harbor facing page top, and shingled storage sheds line the shores of Broad Cove facing page bottom.

NOVA SCOTIA

The shipping boom was to last through the turbulent days of the American Civil War, but, ironically, finally foundered thanks to the enterprise of another Nova Scotian, Samuel Cunard, whose iron steamships were to put an end to billowing sails and yard arms.

Although wooden ships and iron men are a thing of the past, it is a past that Halifax has carefully preserved at Citadel Hill, a splendid star-shaped stone fortress with a commanding view of Halifax and its harbor. Constructed from 1825 to 1856, on the site of an earlier fortification begun in 1749, Citadel Hill bristles with cannon and other impressive war machinery, although no battles have ever been fought for her or around her. Traditionally, the fort's guns go off to announce Royal births and deaths and other events calling for pomp and ceremony.

On the slopes of Citadel Hill is Halifax's Old Town Clock, which tolls each quarter hour with a different peal. Built in 1803 on the order of Prince Edward, Duke of Kent, the tower is circular in shape, in deference to His Royal Highness, who had a penchant for circular architecture as well as punctuality. Other reminders of the Prince's presence in Halifax are the Martello Tower in Point Pleasant Park, and the Prince's Lodge, the remnant of the country home he built for his love, Madame Julie de St Laurent, on a promontory overlooking Bedford Basin. Duty finally compelled the Prince to put aside the lovely Julie (and Halifax), marry a princess, and sire an heir – that most moral of Victorians, Queen Victoria herself.

The Historic Projects reconstruction project encompasses the old waterfront section of Halifax bounded by Granville, Hollis, and Lower Water Streets. To wander along the old cobbled streets is to relive the dying days of the Napoleonic era, the brigandage of the War of 1812, the rough grasp of navy press gangs, and the romance of the windjammers. Everything is much as it was, with one agreeable exception: there are now some tantalizing restaurants and smart shops tucked tastefully into the old warehouses and storage sheds.

Moored frequently at the wharf nearby is *Bluenose II*, a splendid replica of the famous fishing schooner that won so many international races during the 1920s and 1930s and was finally lost off Haiti in 1946. *Bluenose II* is also a

The little fishing community of Tiverton right and above *is located on Long Island, part of a narrow broken finger of land which points in a south-western direction from Digby on the Bay of Fundy. Brilliant blue skies are reflected in the waters of Clarks Harbour* facing page top, *the southernmost town of the province of Nova Scotia. Hacketts Cove is pictured* facing page center; *and* facing page bottom *a view of the enchanting village of Mahone Bay which lies a few miles southwest of Halifax.*

Overleaf The colors, and the quality of light which bathes these fishing villages in the summer months, attract artists, photographers and holiday makers from all over the world. Pictured here is Cape St. Mary in southwestern Nova Scotia.

reminder that while Halifax was busy doing its duty as the "Warden of the Honor of the North" as Kipling dubbed her, the rest of the province went about its less noisy business of fishing and farming.

Nova Scotia is a sea-lover's delight. From the Lighthouse Trails south of Lunenburg, to the record high tides of the Minas Basin on the Bay of Fundy; from Digby, the southern entrance to the Annapolis Valley, with its smoked herring, or "Digby chicks," and its large scallop fleet, to the south shore where much-photographed Peggy's Cove and every little inlet has a tale to tell of wrecks and storms, privateers and the thrill of rum running to the United States during prohibition in the "thirsty" twenties – no place in Nova Scotia is far from the ocean, and its influence is felt on almost everything Nova Scotians do – even farming.

Long before Colonel Cornwallis dug the foundations for Halifax, French settlers in and around the Annapolis Valley and the Minas Basin had devised an elaborate series of dikes for holding back the waters of the Bay of Fundy and ultimately transforming the salt marshlands into fertile farming soil. These French farmers were called Acadians. Their settlements, known as l'Acadie, were founded in 1605 by Samuel de Champlain. The Acadians were diligent farmers, and their well-tended lands eventually attracted the envy of the colonists in neighboring New England.

Pawns in the struggle between France and England for control over North America, the Acadians were forced to leave l'Acadie in 1755 and were transported to New England and other English colonies further south. *Le grand dérangement* is commemorated at Grand Pré, one of the sites of the great exodus, which was immortalized, albeit not quite accurately, by Longfellow in his poem "Evangeline." Fortunately for Nova Scotia, many Acadians made their way back to the province and today their descendants make up about ten percent of Nova Scotia's population.

Shortly after the Acadian expulsion from the Annapolis Valley, the area was settled first by New Englanders, then by Loyalists. Finding the soil rich and the climate mild, these settlers planted apple trees, a practice continued by their descendants. The result makes spring in the Annapolis Valley a fragrant delight of delicate white blossoms.

Eighteenth century upheavals on the North American continent were matched by upheavals abroad. In 1763 the *Hector* disembarked the first Scottish immigrants in Pictou. In the following decades, a flood of dispossessed Scottish crofters and their families made their way to Nova Scotia. Settling all along the Northumberland Strait, they found a land as wild and beautiful as the old home – truly it was a "New Scotland."

Scottish traditions and that hearty zest for life so characteristic of the Scottish temperament are strongly evident in Nova Scotia. They carry on in the skirl of the bagpipes and the flying feet of the young girls at the annual highland games that have been held at Antigonish every year since 1863. And at Pictou, the stone and brick houses with their odd-shaped chimney pots and three-sided dormer windows speak of northern Scotland – as if the scenery and the highland accents to be heard on the streets were not evidence enough.

The repository of Scottish lore, language, and

NOVA SCOTIA

tradition is the Gaelic College at St. Anns, Cape Breton. The only college of its kind in North America, St. Anns teaches young Nova Scotians the Gaelic language and all the age-old crafts of Scotland, as well as hosting the Gaelic Mod, a celebration of the old country, each summer.

Cape Breton is also home to many Nova Scotia Scots whose forebears settled in the hills and valleys that skirt the shore of beautiful Bras d'Or Lake. A deep inland sea, well known to sailors as a safe haven, the tideless lake almost slices Cape Breton neatly in two.

Alexander Graham Bell, who built his summer home *Beinn Breagh* (Gaelic for "beautiful mountain") at Baddeck overlooking Bras d'Or Lake, considered Cape Breton's simple beauty to be unsurpassed anywhere in the world. And if the loch country of Bras d'Or does not bear out the veracity of Bell's opinion, a drive along Cape Breton's ocean highway, the Cabot Trail, certainly will.

Spectacular at any season, but perhaps most captivating in fall when the scarlets and golds of the island's forests flaunt their beauty at the deep blue of the sea and the white of the coastal bluffs, the Cabot Trail is almost 200 miles of awe inspiring natural beauty. More than half the trail winds through the Cape Breton Highlands National Park, an unspoiled wilderness whose rugged landscape tells of long ago upheavals deep within the earth and of the land's fairly recent release from the frigid grasp of the last great Ice Age. Hidden away in the park's interior is the Everlasting Barren, a remote and silent world of muskeg, deep ponds, heath barrens, and twisted, wind-battered spruce.

Pleasure boats and working boats float side by side in the harbor at Cape St. Mary facing page below *and at Short Beach* top right. *Fresh lobster, a gourmet's delight, is plentiful in the clear waters which lap the shores of Nova Scotia, and the lobster traps can be seen piled up on the beach of Indian Harbour* center right *and Sandford Harbour pictured* facing page top and below right. Right *an isolated fishing boat at Poirierville on the Isle Madame.*

The island of Cape Breton became part of Nova Scotia in 1820, but it was only in 1955 that the mainland and the island were finally joined by the construction of the Canso Causeway. The building of the causeway created a deep, ice-free Atlantic anchorage capable of handling large ocean-going vessels. As a result, the causeway complex has opened up a new era of industrial prosperity both for the mainland and for Cape Breton.

With discoveries of oil off the shores of Sable Island, southeast of Halifax, the causeway complex with its large oil refineries at Point Tupper seems likely to be the linchpin in the revitalized industrial front of Nova Scotia.

Cape Breton, unlike the rest of Atlantic Canada, has a very old heavy-industrial base. The Sydney-Glace Bay Area, on Cape Breton's eastern coast, boasts a highly sophisticated industrial workforce with roots going back to the early eighteenth century. This part of Cape Breton

is rich in coal. As a result, Cape Breton's history parallels more that of the great coal-mining areas of England, Scotland, and Wales than the fishing, farming, trading pattern that has always predominated in the Atlantic provinces.

It is a history of great hardship, danger, and callous exploitation. It is also a history of men and women who never gave up their bitter struggle to secure a better life for their children.

The past is never forgotten in this part of Cape Breton. Old mines like the Princess Colliery at Sydney Mines, though now defunct, have been preserved as mining museums. With retired miners to guide you, it is possible to follow the original shaft to the bottom of the pit, which stretches almost a mile under the Atlantic Ocean. Little wonder mining men here are called the men of "the Deeps!" And any older miner can easily tell you stories of boys of nine or ten working down in the pits; of explosions and cave-ins; of the struggle to unionize; of lockouts and strikes and murders – for not that long ago such were the common experiences of men who passed more of their lives in the darkness than in the light.

Port Morien, south of Glace Bay, is the site of the first coal mine in Cape Breton, and probably North America. Here, in 1720, the French started to mine for coal needed for their fortress town of Louisbourg, situated on the southeastern tip of Cape Breton.

Voltaire called Louisbourg the key to France's possessions in North America. No one agreed more than the English who, while waiting for the right moment to unlock the key and take France's fish and furs for themselves, built their own fortress town of Halifax.

The right moment finally came in 1758. The supposedly impregnable fortress fell to a superior force of 15,000 English soldiers. Two years later, with control over the continent assured, the English destroyed Louisbourg.

Two centuries were to pass before the fortress rose again in a masterly restoration undertaken by the federal government. Today, soldiers in eighteenth century uniforms drill again on the parade square, servant wenches gossip on their way to market, and the governor and m'lady and their guests are to be seen whiling away their evenings at the gaming tables as they did so many years ago. The worthy wives of the town again try to coax their gardens into productive life, in patient defiance of the salty mists that sweep in from the ocean. Down by the waterfront at the Hôtel de la Marine, the bitter-sweet taste of cloves as always manages to give *côtelettes de mouton en harcot* that certain special piquancy . . .

Nova Scotians understand the importance of roots. Their awareness of their past, and their pride in it, give them confidence in their future.

An Atlantic storm is forewarned by this ominous gathering of clouds over a little Nova Scotian fishing cove left. The sea has that almost sinister stillness which has come to be known as the calm before the storm. Anyone who loves the sea will love the beautiful province of Nova Scotia, for nowhere is very far from the ocean. Steeped in legend, folklore and, of course, history, each and every cove has its own story to tell . . .

NOVA SCOTIA/PRINCE EDWARD ISLAND

Prince Edward Island

Almost every twelve-year-old girl from Tokyo to London knows *Anne of Green Gables*. Anne, of the red hair and freckles, irrepressible spirit and twenty-four-hour tongue, the little orphan from Nova Scotia who was sent by mistake to Prince Edward Island and stayed to delight the skeptical Islanders and, inadvertently, put P.E.I. on the map.

Canada's smallest province, P.E.I. stretches a mere 140 miles from North Cape to East Point, or as the indigenous Micmac Indians called it, "Kespemanagek," the end of the island. No matter where you are on Prince Edward Island, the ocean is never more than ten miles away. At its narrowest, P.E.I. is just four miles wide. Where the sea has made the least inroad, only forty miles separate coast from coast. In between lies a miniature paradise – an Atlantic Elysium that each year attracts thousands of visitors who come to play in her brilliant blue waters, bask on her golden sandy beaches, delight in the splendid harvest the Islanders extract from the sea, and find peace in the unhurried rural round of the island's sociable citizens.

On the whole, nature has always been rather indulgent toward P.E.I. The island is subject to some quite wide temperature fluctuations, owing to the eastward movement of air masses from the North American continent to the Atlantic Ocean. But to offset this minor inconvenience, moist air from the ocean makes sure island winters are bearable and the summers bewitching.

Even the earth's bygone convulsions conspired to benefit P.E.I., sometimes at the expense of her neighbors.

In the northeastern part of the province of Nova Scotia is Cape Breton Island these pages. Igonish facing page bottom right is a harbor village situated in the Cape Breton Highlands National Park. The park comprises a huge tableland, a rugged Atlantic coastline, and a hilly forested area. From the Cabot Trail can be seen magnificent views of the sea, and the park is well provided with camping facilities and local accommodation. Neils Harbour above right and facing page top left lies a few miles north of Igonish, its lobster traps, lighthouse and fishing boats making a pretty picture in the sunlight. The elegant building facing page top right and bottom left is the Fortress of Louisbourg in the National Historic Park, west of Louisbourg and south of Sydney. The flower-filled meadow right, at St. Peter's, is typical of the gently undulating countryside to be found throughout the province of Nova Scotia.

Breton, and Quebec. This clay soil, stained reddish brown by the iron oxide trapped in the bedrock below, goes deep down into the bowels of the island. Although acidic and somewhat low on nutrient, it can be encouraged to yield abundantly.

To nourish the island's soil, some early farmers used to cover their fields with alluvial mud containing mussels and other shellfish. Farmers nearer the coast would wait for Atlantic storms to deposit oyster and lobster shells on shore, which were then garnered and transported inland

Offspring of the ancient Canadian Shield, the island began its formation as sediment drained into the Gulf of St. Lawrence from the mountains of the shield about 200 million years ago. Countless centuries in the making, the island results from the layering of salt and sediment on the bottom of the gulf. One other vital ingredient went into making this rocky layer-cake – iron oxide (rust) – which was to stain the sandstone of P.E.I. a vibrant rusty red.

Like the rest of Atlantic Canada, present day Prince Edward Island owes its shape and form to the Wisconsin Glacier. The island received the earth scraped up by the glacier as it ground its way across New Brunswick, Cape

to spread over the soil. Either way, come spring plowing, these rich deposits were crushed, adding precious lime and nutrients to the earth.

Farming today does not call for quite as much exertion, but it is a busy life. To make the most of the growing season, crops like tobacco, raised in the east of the island, are started early in greenhouses. A thriving dairy industry keeps Islanders in milk and cheese, and there is enough left over to send to the mainland. Grain is grown widely across Prince Edward Island, both for animal and human consumption. Vegetables of all kinds bring in a ready source of cash for farming families. And as any visitor to P.E.I. will tell you, nothing rivals island strawberries for their sinful succulence, except perhaps the juicy wild blueberries, which have been known to turn the most genteel into ravaging gluttons.

But the "Garden of the Gulf" won its name not from its broccoli or blueberries, but from its early development of the potato. Not long ago, Prince Edward Island was literally "Spud Island," with farmers concentrating almost exclusively on potato growing. The market for spuds is notoriously fickle, and sole reliance on the potato has given way now to less risky mixed farming. Lest anyone think the potato has lost its pride of place in island agriculture, however, one of P.E.I.'s biggest traffic jams – the wait for the mainland ferry notwithstanding – occurs each fall at Summerside, the island's second largest community, when truck after truck laden with "Bud the Spud" clog the streets waiting to unload their cargo onto potato boats moored in the harbor in the center of town.

If Islanders do not make a living from the land it is likely they do from the sea. Here the lobster, that strange crustacean left over from the age of the dinosaur, holds sway. No lobster ever dies of old age, runs an old maxim down east, and given the relentless pursuit of these ungainly but delectable creatures, it is no wonder. Although prolific breeders, lobsters have not been able to keep up with demand. To make sure the lobster stock does not become depleted, P.E.I. fishermen must be licensed to trap lobster, and may only do so in accordance with

eat the oysters raw. (Any Islander will be pleased to provide shucking instructions!)

Clams, mussels, scallops, Atlantic salmon, and trout – Prince Edward Island has them all, and all are within plate's reach of the laziest visitor. If, however, digging for clams for a beach supper is too slow in pace, rod action awaits the keen fisherman in the blue-fin tuna waters off the North Cape.

The sea's bounty is not limited just to fish. The next time you lick a cone of your favorite ice cream, you are likely consuming a further export from P.E.I.'s waters. Carrageenin, used as a stabilizer in ice cream and many other foods, is the end product of Irish moss, one of the island's most important export crops.

Storms churn up the purplish seaweed from the ocean bottom and carry it to shore. In the wake of a storm, Islanders may be seen in small boats raking the weed into nets, or else wading through the frothy shore breakers gathering the moss as they go. To an onlooker, the scene is reminiscent of Synge or Yeats: the men with their long-handled rakes; the horse standing harnessed to the old open wagon at water's edge, waiting patiently to haul off the dripping load; scudding clouds above; sulky sea behind; and only a shy sun to help take the nip out of the air. More than half of the world's Irish moss comes from Prince Edward Island.

But if the sea and the land provide Prince Edward Island with sustenance, it is the island's varied scenery – a

government regulations.

Nothing is more evocative of island life than tranquil harbors with small boats moored snugly at day's end – the last rays of a fading sun mirroring the neat piles of wooden lobster traps, aligned like so many portable homes along the wharf. And as for the flavor of P.E.I., why, it is best savored at one of the numerous lobster suppers held in church halls and community centers across the island.

In addition to lobsters, Prince Edward Island offers discriminating gourmets a further taste delight – the Malpeque oyster. Those in the know consider Malpeque oysters to be the world's best, an opinion, incidentally, also held by Islanders. All island oysters are called Malpeques, whether they originate in beautiful Malpeque Bay to the north of Summerside, or in any of the smaller inlets. Aficionados usually "shuck," or shell, their Malpeques and

Peggy's Cove above, above left and facing page is a very typical Nova Scotian fishing village. It is extremely popular with visitors who come to see its spindle-legged dock, its weathered boats, its bleached rocks and its attractive lighthouse. As with most towns and villages on the Atlantic coast, Peggy's Cove is subject to unpredictable weather conditions, and violent storms buffet the rocks, houses and boats which at the moment look so peaceful. Stormy skies threaten Blue Rocks left.

magnet to visitors – that gives Islanders their spending money.

Jacques Cartier, the first European to visit the island, wrote of Prince Edward Island: "It is the best-tempered region one can possibly see…Nothing is wanting but harbors." Much of the mighty forests Cartier saw that July of 1534 have gone, victims of fire, settlement, and an early period of shipbuilding. And, of course, nature had endowed the island with copious inlets and bays, which Cartier failed to observe because of the many sandbars and dunes that are the first sign of land to be seen from the sea.

Squabbled and fought over by both France and England, the island, at various times known as Île St. Jean, St. John's Island, New Ireland, and Abegweit, the Micmac for a land cradled on the waves, was finally named for Prince Edward, Duke of Kent, father of Queen Victoria. In its long history it has suffered the abuse of absentee landlords, indifferent colonial rule, pirate raids, and plagues of mice that reduced her people to starvation. But whether dispossessed Scottish crofters, resolute Acadians determined to retain their language and culture in face of cruel deportation, displaced Loyalists, or Quakers fleeing the intolerance of more established religions, Islanders have always been steadfast people and as such have not only endured, but left their stamp on their unique home.

It is quite possible to see P.E.I. by bicycle or on foot. The more impatient may drive, although a word of caution is advised. No, it is not the roads; they are excellent. And it is impossible to get lost on the island. The crookedest byway eventually winds its way back to a main road, and the three counties rival each other in the beauty of their well-mapped scenic routes – Lady Slipper Drive in Prince, Blue Heron Drive in Queens, and King's Byway in Kings. Actually, it is P.E.I. itself: It defies the itinerary-conscious motorist to keep on schedule. Just waiting for the ferry to bring you, and your car, either from Cape Tormentine in New Brunswick to Borden, or from Caribou in Nova Scotia to Wood Islands, is excellent preparation for entry to a society where rush and stress just do not hold sway.

Once on P.E.I., you will appreciate why tranquillity is the pervading mood of the island. Prince Edward Island is a land for the senses: from the sweet vapor that rises from the red clay as spring's warmth is felt on the land, to the salt tang in the sea air; from the trees blindingly bedecked in the golds and reds of fall, to the menacing white icebergs that each winter glide imperiously through the Northumberland Strait; from the soft pink of a delicate Lady Slipper orchid sheltering on the mossy forest floor to the brassy red of the cliffs dipping into the azure of the sea; from skittish colts to the scraping of fiddles at a country dance. Everything on Prince Edward Island seems just the same today as when young Anne and her friends romped and played at Avonlea back before World War I upset the century.

In some ways, though, this unchanging tranquillity is deceptive. The elements are constantly at work slowly remoulding and reshaping the island. To wander along the shore at North Cape is to experience a world constantly on the move. Here, where red sandstone cliffs meet the

Peggy's Cove sparkles with color in the summer sunshine left. *The water is calm, and* *lobster traps can be seen drying on the jetty.*

225

NOVA SCOTIA/PRINCE EDWARD ISLAND

Only about five percent of Nova Scotia's land is suitable for growing crops, and most of the agriculture is based on livestock, poultry and dairy farming. Fishing is a major activity and the province has many lovely fishing villages like Peggy's Cove these pages. Shellfish, haddock and cod are the main catches.

About one-eighth of Nova Scotia's population is descended from Acadian French, while the remainder are mostly descended from English and Scottish settlers. Along the coastal areas, many families combine farming and

fishing for lobsters and ground fish, especially along the southern and the southwestern shores which have milder and wetter climates than the remainder of the province.

merging Northumberland Strait and the tides of the Gulf of St. Lawrence, the many caves, arches, and crevices in the cliff-face bear testimony to the triumph of water over rock. In this age-old contest, the rock is no match for the constant onslaught of the sea, whether it be summer's nibbling breakers or winter's ice-maddened sprays. About three feet of sandstone are lost to the sea each year, and the lighthouse that beams a warning to ships as well as the road leading to the cape are both relocated on occasion to keep a jump ahead of the marching sea.

A less spectacular but nevertheless unending destruction can occur on the beaches of central and eastern Prince Edward Island, the most famous of which is Cavendish. The ocean's gift to the island, the beaches are sheltered by sand dunes, themselves the product of sand washed ashore by the ocean. The task of holding fast the dunes falls to *Ammophilia arenaria*, the marram grass. Sending its long roots probing deep down into the sand, the marram grass does a remarkable job of stabilizing the dunes. Unfortunately, just when the grass is most dry and brittle and vulnerable, it is most likely to be heedlessly assaulted by visitors unaware of its significance in the island's ecosystem. Should the marram grass lose its restraining grasp on the dunes, the sands would spread over the fields and choke the fishing harbors. Needless to say, the unspoken watchword around P.E.I.'s beaches is:

Enjoy yourself, but keep off the grass!

A sense of responsible civic-mindedness also pervades P.E.I.'s gracious old capital, Charlottetown, home to about 20,000 Islanders.

Charlottetown's foundations were laid by the French in the early 1700s, in recognition, no doubt, of her excellent harbor. In those days the community was known as Port LaJoye. When George III annexed the then Île St. Jean to England in 1763, the task of establishing a capital in His Majesty's newest colony fell to Captain Samuel Holland, Surveyor-General of all British possessions north of the Potomac River. Satisfied with the French choice, Holland renamed Port LaJoye in honor of King George's patient spouse, Queen Charlotte.

Charlottetown will always endure as the site of an event of great importance in the evolution of the Canadian nation. For it was here on September 1, 1864, that the Fathers of Confederation arrived on the *Queen Victoria*, the "Confederation Cruiser," to lay the foundations for the Canada we know today.

Today, the old legislative building, site of that memorable meeting, must also share pride of place with a much newer edifice – the Charlottetown Confederation Centre. Built in 1964 as a national "thank you" to the Fathers of Confederation, it houses a memorial hall, an gallery, museum, library, and theater.

And each year, thousands of sunburned kids leave the beaches for a brief while to come to the theater to see "Anne of Green Gables," that marvellous musical retelling of L. M. Montgomery's beloved story. Like the Fathers of Confederation, long red country roads, yellow buttercups, sweet lobsters, and fields of spuds, Anne is a part of the island. If anything, she is the spirit of unspoiled innocence that is the very essence of Prince Edward Island itself.

PRINCE EDWARD ISLAND

Pictured on these pages is Canada's smallest province, Prince Edward Island. Charlottetown is the province's capital as well as being its only city. Affectionately nicknamed "the birthplace of Canada," it was here that the Fathers of Confederation met for the first time in September 1864. Charlottetown's Legislative Building can be seen bottom right. The island has some exceptionally fine sandy *beaches, some of which are dominated by towering red sandstone cliffs. The coastal scenery is as beautiful as it is varied right, facing page, below where a ship is shown leaving the Borden ferry terminal, and bottom where lobster traps are piled high on the beach. The attractive weatherboarded house center right, situated near Cavendish, was immortalized in Lucy Maud Montgomery's book, "Anne of Green Gables."*

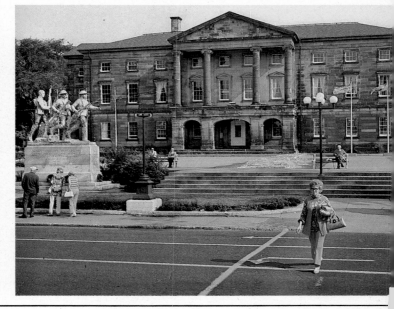

NEWFOUNDLAND AND LABRADOR

Newfoundland's wealth is in the seas around her. For almost 500 years her Grand Banks have teemed with fish, bringing the world's fishing fleets to her rocky shores. Now the ocean promises her a new source of wealth – oil. At Hibernia, 190 miles southeast of St. John's, the offshore oil and gas discoveries equal some twenty-seven percent of Canada's current conventional reserves.

These days, there is an air of expectant bustle and change in St. John's. Looking down over the old capital from Signal Hill, near the spot where Marconi received the first trans-Atlantic wireless signals back in 1901, St. John's spreads – comfortable, settled, and hitherto unhurried – around the deep, landlocked harbor that has been a haven to shipping for centuries. The changes taking place show in her skyline and in her harbor. Tall office towers and hotels have overtaken the spires of the venerable Anglican cathedral, the oldest example of Gothic church architecture in North America, and dwarf the charming Victorian buildings and the brightly painted frame houses built when the century was young.

The harbor itself tells the tale of the transformation of St. John's. Once small boys used to play hooky to greet the incoming Portuguese fishing fleet. Now the harbor's great attractions are the drilling rigs.

Fortunately, though, for all its new buildings, suburban development, and the changing face of its harbor, the ghosts of old St. John's still make their presence felt. Water Street, the oldest street in North America, is perhaps their favorite haunt.

When Sir Humphrey Gilbert dropped anchor in St. John's harbor in 1583 to claim Newfoundland for Elizabeth I, he found a community of fishermen from England, France, Portugal and Spain already established there. Trade with England, the West Indies, and the English colonies along the Atlantic seaboard increased St. John's importance and her population over the centuries. Rum, fish, sealskins, wine, food stuffs, and all manner of trade goods were stored in the Water Street warehouses of such wealthy mercantile concerns as Bowring Brothers, Job & Company, Robert & Thomas Newman, and Crosbie and Company. Today, the Water Street merchants no longer dispense a daily tot of rum to each employee, but their business empires still reach out from Water Street to distant ports around the globe.

Aeons ago, the island of Newfoundland was part of the North American land mass. But millions of years of geological upheaval caused the separation of the island from the mainland. Newfoundland's rugged coastline is a legacy of the great Wisconsin Glacier which covered the land some 20,000 years ago. As the ice moved toward the boundless sea, it carved the countless deep bays and fjords that are such a feature of the island.

By the time Bjarni Herjulfesson and his Viking adventurers sighted the coast of Newfoundland and Labrador a thousand years ago, the stately hemlock forests that covered the land told them this was not the treeless Greenland they had planned to visit. Later, other Viking explorers settled at the site of present-day L'Anse-aux-Meadows. Here, at the very northern tip of Newfound-

Newfoundland is Canada's tenth and newest province and, until 1949, was Britain's oldest colony. Scores of fishing villages cling to its rugged shores, and fishing fleets from all over the world harvest its waters.

land, today accessible either by road or coastal ferry, the traces of that long-ago Viking settlement may be seen and explored by tourists and historians.

The lonely isolation of L'Anse-aux-Meadows accentuates the necessity of the work of the late Dr. Wilfred Grenfell and his mission based in the nearby town of St. Anthonys. His desire to bring medical care to the farflung communities of northern Newfoundland and Labrador led Dr. Grenfell to found the mission in 1892.

It is to Britain and Ireland, not the Vikings, that the island's citizens look for their roots. Indeed, so strong is this heritage that the speech of Newfoundlanders today is still liberally laced with terms and expressions not heard in County Clare or Devon for a hundred years.

Almost five centuries have passed since the navigator John Cabot came ashore at Cape Bonavista in 1497, mistaking the "new founde lande" for the farthest reaches of Tartary. Hoping to find a western route to the Orient, Cabot sailed along the coast in the tiny ship *Matthew*, scanning Newfoundland's seemingly impenetrable forests for just a glimpse of the gold-topped roofs of Peking, described two hundred years before by Marco Polo. Cabot never did find gossamer silks, pungent perfumes, or exotic spices to take back to Henry VII of England. But when he returned home with tales of waters teeming with fish, no doubt Henry was not altogether disappointed.

Catholic Europe, with its many meatless days of religious observation, was a prime market for fish. Moreover, Europeans were moving from their farms and the prospect of a plentiful, and cheap, source of food for the growing cities caused much interest in the courts of Europe.

It has been said that the Grand Banks are Newfoundland's lost fertility. Whether or not the Wisconsin Glacier carried the good earth of Newfoundland along on its unheeding flow to the sea is unproven. What is sure is that the banks, lying just southeast of Newfoundland, are the recipients of an expansive nature's generosity. An extension of the continental shelf running down the coast of North America, the Grand Banks lie at a depth of about thirty-five fathoms, an ideal habitat for the many schools of fish that feed there. The sun smiles upon the banks, which are further warmed by the lifegiving Gulf Stream. From the north, the cool Labrador Current washes over them, bringing with it the plankton so essential to the fertility of the banks. Incidentally, this mixing of Gulf Stream and Labrador Current is responsible for the famous smothering, grey, dripping, enveloping Newfoundland fogs. On a "mausey" day you cannot see your hand before your very face, so thick is the fog.

For centuries fishermen from Spain, Portugal, France and England have braved the ill-humored Atlantic to come and fill their nets and baskets with cod. Of these hardy men of the sea, naught remains but the place names which tell of their origin – Portugal Cove, Harbor Breton, Ireland's Eye, Jersey Harbor – and a priceless legacy of feisty independence which their heirs maintain to this day.

Pictured left is a sea of logs, at Stephenville on the western shore of Newfoundland. Lumbering is one of the province's major industries, *alongside fishing. The Newfoundland fisheries are the most productive in the world, cod being the most important variety.*

NEWFOUNDLAND AND LABRADOR

Stand on a wharf in a fishing cove or outport anywhere along the coast, with the sun shining above and the waves slapping mischievously onto the shore, and watch the men put to sea; it is impossible to imagine a more tranquil scene. With the gossipy activity of the outport at your back, the gulls bossy and active overhead, and the energetic maneuverings of the small boats before you, the hardships that centuries of Newfoundland folk have endured in the quest for a livelihood seem unbelievable.

Witness a full-fledged Atlantic storm, a rage of marching black clouds, with rain fierce enough to batter a strong man to his knees, winds howling and shrieking out of the east, driving the waves ashore to explode in sheets of venomous spray, and it is hard to grasp how anyone, fish or no fish, would want to live on this ancient rock. Newfoundlanders see things differently.

To an islander, there is the pride of having stood before the rage of wind and sea for generation after generation; the knowledge of having weathered the squabbles of great powers; and the satisfaction of having survived the greed of avaricious merchants who for centuries controlled the market for fish. Pirates, ghosts, inefficient government, and assorted lesser evils have likewise all been taken in stride.

In 1948, the island voted, at long last, to join the Canadian Confederation. Confederation brought roads, better ferry services, needed schools, and electricity to the outports, and ended their centuries-old isolation. Today, Newfoundland is easily reached by plane, or by the ferry that daily crosses from North Sydney, Nova Scotia, to Port aux Basques.

Long-johns still dry, frozen and funny, on outdoor winter clotheslines, and the coarse oily-wool socks that Newfoundland women have been knitting for their men for as long as can be remembered, may still be seen atop fence palings, the better to dry in the stiff sea breeze. But older Newfoundlanders bemoan the passing of the good old days. While no one sighs for the back-wrenching days of rowboats; or of summers spent turning the split cod as they dried on high wooden platforms, or flakes; or of an everlasting diet of fish, brewis, and pease pudding (boiled salt cod, with hardtack biscuit soaked in water, and a side helping of mashed split peas), still there was a warmth and comfort of belonging in your own, unique community which, to those in the know, does not quite exist any more. Screech, they will tell you, is not quite as good either; although to the uninitiated a gulp of this potent Newfie rum is liable to cause a violent storm in gullet and gut alike. Reels and gigs are not quite as lively, or the yarns as fanciful as when they were young, but then that is just the opinion of the pre-forty-niners, the islanders who remain unabashedly and cheerfully Newfoundlanders first, and Canadians second. Their children, they will tell you, think differently.

Young Newfoundlanders are, as always, on the go; whether off to seek their fortune in the Alberta boom cities of Calgary and Edmonton, or at work on the province's own resource-based industries – the fish-processing plants; the pulp and newsprint mills at Corner Brook, Newfoundland's chief industrial center, and now in the offshore quest for oil and gas.

Newfoundland also has a new industry – tourism. There is a rugged timeless beauty about the land that both soothes and invigorates jaded urbanites. In addition to the island's fine beaches and great fishing, Newfoundland's awesome wilderness parks – Terra Nova in the far east, and Gros Morne in the somber Long Range Mountains along the northwest coast, are home to herds of caribou, Newfoundland's provincial animal. Black bear, lynx, ermine, river otter, beaver, pine marten, red fox, moose, and the shy arctic hare are also to be found in their natural habitat in the parks.

The indomitable cliffs of Burgeo and Fortune Bay provide remote homes for both the mighty bald eagle and the golden eagle. If there is one sight that captures the essence of the island's spirit, it is a great bald eagle soaring high above craggy cliffs and sparkling fjords – master of its own destiny. The rest of Newfoundland's bird population, puffins, ptarmigans, gannets, murres, kittiwake gulls, and other species all find a safe haven on Newfoundland's

three bird sanctuaries: in Witless Bay, Cape St. Mary's, and on Funk Island, where they build their nests on every available perch in a manner rather reminiscent of the outporters' own cliff-hugging houses. So dense is the covering of birds in these sanctuaries, that fishermen claim the incredible sound of so many mating, parenting birds is enough to drive a person mad; that is, if one could abide the smell long enough for the assault on one's ears to take effect. Needless to say, the phosphate and nitrate rich droppings deposited by these colonies run to hundreds of thousands of tons each year, and are an invaluable contribution to the abundance of plankton on the Grand Banks.

For a total step backward in geological time, a visit to Labrador is a must. Tell a Newfoundlander that you are taking the ferry from Black Duck Cove across the Strait of Belle Isle to Labrador and, in addition to being cautioned to take winter underwear and mittens, no matter what the season, you will probably receive Newfoundland's view of Labrador's creation. The old saying is that God made Labrador in six days, and on the seventh He threw stones at it. Labrador does nothing to dispel this opinion. Covering 112,826 square miles (Newfoundland itself is only 43,359 square miles), Labrador offers vistas of aching severity. Undeniably, Newfoundland itself has mighty cliffs, deep fjords, and forests so silent and stern that even a whisper seems sacrilegious, but in Labrador all these

NEWFOUNDLAND AND LABRADOR

There are many fishing towns and villages along the Newfoundland coast which are known as "outports," such as Port aux Basques facing page. Fishing is a mainstay of the economy, and angling is a very popular sport, both inland and at sea. Waters are alive with speckled brook, rainbow and brown trout, and Atlantic salmon. People come from all over the world to fish for 600-pound bluefin tuna, which they haul in, on rod and line, from Conception Bay. Newfoundland juts out into the Atlantic so far east that its clocks are 1½ hours ahead of New York time! This point, close to historic St. John's, can be reached by ferry from Nova Scotia, the journey taking about six hours.

Below *Logs being transported to the pulp mills – a major source of congestion in Newfoundland's waterways.*

natural wonders are just so much higher, deeper, and more brooding. It is the excess of the land that overwhelms, and to really experience this tumultuous handiwork of nature, you must travel up the coast on one of the small vessels that take supplies to Labrador's scattered outports.

As the fog and mist press in around you, blotting out the rocky headlands, you find yourself peering intently into the stillness, half expecting to see the prow of a Viking longboat defiantly breasting the waters toward you, so unchanged over the centuries is this unruly land. The trip, like Labrador itself, is always full of surprises. Buffeted by a singularly unpleasant sea in the open waters around Cape Harrison, and drenched in spume whipped up by the 50 to 60 knot winds, you cannot help wondering why you came at all! But on a "loomy" day, when the shifts in the density of air above the water play havoc with the light's rays, islands, seeming to hang suspended in mid-air, suddenly loom before you, although, in fact, they are below the horizon. It is a sight of such tantalizing beauty that all soakings and seasickness are worth it!

Where once only the native Inuit hunted the vast caribou herds and fishermen eked out a meager existence, and a few Moravian missionaries struggled to bring education and religion to both, Labrador's natural resources have now nudged the region into prosperity. The mighty Churchill River has been harnessed to provide hydro electricity, and the iron-ore mines in the west have led to the growth of lively new towns like Labrador City and Wabush. Old ways die hard, however, and both fishing and sealing, a controversial occupation in Newfoundland and Labrador, continue.

Will the prosperity brought by oil spoil the ancient charms of Newfoundland and Labrador? That is the question her citizens are asking with a mixture of hope for the future and love of their heritage. It is still too early to tell. Although a land seemingly indestructible, the stern visage of the region is really just a cover for an extremely fragile ecosystem. Previous unchecked progress has claimed many casualties: the Boethuk Indians proved no match for the ruthlessly acquisitive Europeans, who succeeded in destroying them totally. The great auk and Labrador duck now exist only in the splendid paintings of Audubon. There are some positive signs, however. The extending of Canada's boundaries to take in 200 miles of ocean is a first step at heading off the depletion of the sea's bounty. Interest in the province's history and culture is high among young Newfoundlanders – a promising portent for the future.

For the present, fishermen still watch to see if the herring gulls fly high, an indication of stormy weather, before heading out into open water. And in St. John's as well as the outports, mummers still don their centuries-old crazy garb and entertain from door-to-door at Christmas. Great icebergs, like so many Grand Hotels, still sail majestically down the Strait of Belle Isle – Iceberg Alley, as it is known – en route to oblivion in the warmer climes to the south.

To Newfoundlanders, come good times or bad, it is still always "fish in summer, and fun in winter." Everything in its place!

St. John's is Newfoundland's capital, and the continent's closest city to Europe. It was from here that, in 1901,

Marconi received the first trans-Atlantic wireless signal. Overleaf The snowbound Northwest Territories.

THE YUKON & THE NORTHWEST TERRITORIES

In 1897, an impressionable young Californian oyster pirate turned tramp turned laundry worker turned mill-hand set off for Dawson City in the Yukon. Only twenty-one, this young man arrived broke but determined to make his fortune in the gold fields of the Klondike. A year later he left, still broke, but with his head full of tales of the strange, wonderful, ruthless world of the Yukon gold rush. Jack London never made his fortune panning for gold, but his experiences in the Yukon, recorded in his short-story collection *The Son of the Wolf* and his bestselling novel *The Call of the Wild*, brought London both fame and fortune, and the Yukon immortality.

When Jack London arrived in Dawson City, Queen Victoria still ruled in England, supervising her subjects' manners and morals with the same close scrutiny she applied to the overseeing of her vast empire. However, as young London soon discovered, the Queen of Dawson City was actually a lady who was a good deal less particular of manners and morality. Diamond Tooth Gertie was, without a doubt, the toast of Dawson City, and her gambling hall was the center of the Yukon's rip-roaring city of gold.

The great Yukon gold rush that centered around Dawson City was like a mighty forest fire. It had started innocuously enough when an American drifter, George Carmack, discovered gold while panning in Rabbit Creek, a small tributary of the Klondike River, during the summer of 1896.

route from Dyea, danger and imminent disaster kept step with them all the way. The White Pass trail was a treacherous rocky mountain path obstructed by giant boulders. Missed footing meant certain death for man and beast. Eventually, a railway line was pushed through the White Pass, carrying all traffic from Skagway to Whitehorse, the latter a little depot community that served Dawson City.

The Chilkoot trail was no easier, yet some 30,000 gold-hungry men and women travelled it between the winter of 1897 and the fall of '98. When prospectors reached the Alaska-Canada border, the North West Mounted Police – stationed originally in the Yukon at Fortymile mining camp to convince the Americans in neighboring Alaska that the Yukon was actually a part of Canada – insisted that they possess enough supplies to last for one year before they could enter the country. A year's supplies ran to more than 2,000 pounds and was generally carried by miners the hard way – on their backs. Needless to say, getting this awesome load to the other side of the pass necessitated many trips. Just transferring supplies across the Chilkoot Pass, a trip of thirty-three miles one way, usually wound up being a gruelling 1,000 miles.

Once over the pass, the prospectors were called upon to exercise their skills as boatbuilders, for the foot trail ended at Bennett and Lindeman lakes. The Klondike could only be reached by water. The winter was spent

At first glance, nowhere could seem more inhospitable than Canada's northernmost regions, the Northwest Territories and the Yukon. Fierce Arctic winters are accompanied by unbelievably cold temperatures, but when the summer comes, and the north turns into the "land of the midnight sun" temperatures turn mild and the daylight is permanent! Some 18,000 Inuit, often erroneously called Eskimoes, live in Canada, and few nowadays live in igloos – the majority having opted for four solid walls and central heating. Bell Telecommunications facing page top right are based at Frobisher Bay.

Within a month of Carmack's discovery, Rabbit Creek had proved itself worthy of its new name "Bonanza," and 200 new claims had been staked in the area. The following spring, Bonanza's miners, wealthy men all, set sail for Seattle and San Francisco to sell their gold to the United States mints.

Fed by rumors which grew wilder by the hour, men turned prospector overnight, hastily outfitted themselves, and sought passage on ships bound for Skagway or Dyea, on the coast of the Alaska panhandle. Once on land the prospectors had to cross the Coast Mountains to reach the Yukon River and the Klondike gold field.

Whether the would-be millionaires set off from Skagway via the White Pass, or took the Chilkoot Pass

felling timber and fashioning boats. At spring thaw in 1898, over 7,000 hastily built craft were ready to set off on the hazardous 500-mile journey to the Klondike.

Staking a claim was relatively easy; working it was backbreaking. Yet no matter how gruelling the work, as long as tales of gold in the Klondike were to be heard throughout the world, people came to seek their fortune in the Yukon. The rush petered out around 1904, some eight years after Carmack's discovery. During that period, 80,000 people flocked to the area, and over $100 million worth of gold was extracted from the rivers and streams of the Yukon. Much of the money was spent in Dawson City – the boom town that blossomed just where the Yukon and Klondike rivers meet.

At first Dawson City was just a collection of rough

timber shacks and canvas tents. But when her miners struck paydirt, so did Dawson City. The shacks gave way to impressive two-storey edifices, and the stores were soon stocked with fine foods, brandy, cigars, and beautiful dresses for the miners' ladies, a comely bunch of brazen belles who worked the innumerable saloons and taverns which made Dawson City such a haven for weary miners. In the short arctic summer a veritable flotilla of sternwheelers sailed direct to Dawson City, up the Yukon River from the Bering Strait, laden with the luxuries her flush population craved, and bulging with yet more prospectors with gold dust in their eyes.

In its heyday, Dawson City was the Paris of the north but when the gold ran out, miners, can-can dancers, card sharps, confidence tricksters, tailors, dentists, barbers, preachers, all drifted away. Within a very short time, Dawson City was a ghost town.

The wicked, wild Yukon lives on in the stories of Jack London and the poems of Robert Service, the most famous of which, "The Shooting of Dan McGrew," captures Dawson City at its bawdy best. Dawson City has long been eclipsed by Whitehorse, but, thanks to a careful restoration program, today there is fresh life in the old "city of gold."

Sourdough bread and beans may once more be sampled in Dawson City's clapboard taverns, and over at Gambling Gertie's the dice are tossed again, the roulette wheels spin and the can-can dancers kick as high as Gertie's girls once did.

Gold mining is still important to the Yukon. Some $19.5 million worth of ore was extracted in 1981, and silver yielded $101 million in the same period. The giant Anvil mineral development – lead, zinc, gold, silver – northeast of Whitehorse, yields up to forty percent of the Yukon's total yearly earnings.

In his poem, "The Spell of the Yukon," Robert Service told how gold lured him to the Yukon, but some mysterious, intangible quality of the land itself kept him there. Service described the Yukon from ". . . its big, dizzy mountains to its deep deathlike valleys," as the "cussedest" land he knew.

Cussed or not, the Yukon is big. Bounded by Alaska on the west, British Columbia to the south, and the Northwest Territories on the east, the Yukon stretches northward past the Arctic Circle to the Beaufort Sea. It is a mountainous, water-riven wilderness of 207,076 square miles: more than twice the size of Great Britain. And it is cold, though Yukoners will tell you that Siberia is much colder and they defend their much-maligned winters by telling you that if children in prairie towns can brave the chills for a little street hockey before supper, so can children in Whitehorse, because the temperatures are about the same, generally between plus 4° and minus 58°C. Summers are short, but delightfully warm, as outdoor lovers who come north to explore, hike, canoe, and fish will verify.

Most of the Yukon is served by one of three major highways: the Alaska Highway, from Dawson Creek, B.C., to Fairbanks, Alaska; the Klondike Highway, built to transport ore and minerals; and the more recent Dempster Highway, which links Dawson City with Fort McPherson

Snow and ice turn the bare trees into a shimmering network of black and white, and well-insulated cabins nestle under their blankets of snow.

THE YUKON & THE NORTHWEST TERRITORIES

and Inuvik, high in the north on the Mackenzie River delta.

Regular air transport exists between Whitehorse and Vancouver, British Columbia, and Edmonton, Alberta, and ships bring visitors to Skagway, Alaska, whence the rest of the trip may be taken by train.

Yet for all its accessibility and its popularity with visitors wise enough to appreciate the unexpected in holiday adventures, the Yukon is sparsely populated, and perhaps that is one of its great charms. Less than 25,000 people live here, with about 7,000 making their home in the capital, Whitehorse.

At present, the Yukon Territory and the adjacent Northwest Territories do not have provincial status within the Canadian Confederation, although they do elect their own members of parliament who represent them in the House of Commons in Ottawa. Each territory has its own government, with scope over education, local government, public works and the like, as do the provinces in the south, but a federal ministry controls the purse-strings and the federal government has control over most of the natural resources.

Dawson City is the quintessential Yukon of yesterday and Whitehorse the prosperous face of today. But the timeless Yukon is preserved inviolate in wildly beautiful Kluane National Park, situated in the southwest corner of the territory. This great park is dominated by the towering peaks of the St. Elias Mountains, which are, in turn, lorded over by Mount Logan, at 19,850 feet Canada's highest mountain.

There are over 2,000 glaciers in Kluane. Included in this vast number of ice-age souvenirs is the Steele Glacier, which is known to surge forward at an uncommonly rapid rate – for a glacier. In the late 1960s, it slid downhill a distance of seven miles in just four months, earning the nickname of the "galloping glacier."

Kluane is not a frozen waste, however. Forests and alpine tundra, marshes and sand dunes all have their place in the park's ecosystem. Thanks to the influence of the Pacific Ocean, the vegetation in the southeast of the park is quite luxuriant.

Moose graze in Kluane's valleys, and snow-white Dall sheep and mountain goats roam the rocky slopes. Small herds of caribou can be seen near the Duke River. Grizzly bears range everywhere throughout the park, while black bears inhabit the forested areas. Other mammals include wolves, coyotes, red foxes, wolverine, arctic ground squirrels, lynx, beavers, otters, muskrats, minks, marmot, and snowshoe hares. Over 170 species of birds have been reported there.

Kluane glistens with high cresting waterfalls, lovely mountain lakes and gleaming rivers. The park has an extensive trail system for hikers and skiers, and the mountains attract climbers from all over the world. Kluane is definitely a supreme wilderness challenge. Only the very seasoned should venture into the park's interior, for sudden blizzards are not uncommon even in July, and help is usually far away.

Anyone who has experienced Kluane would not find it difficult to understand why Yukoners are fiercely proud of their strange and beautiful land, a land which they, like Robert Service, would trade for no other land on earth.

Bell Telecommunications, whose snow-covered *installations can be seen left, are based at Frobisher Bay.*

THE YUKON & THE NORTHWEST TERRITORIES

Once, the Northwest Territories included all land drained by the rivers flowing into Hudson Bay. This took in segments of present-day northern Ontario and Quebec. The area was reduced to its present size of 1,304,903 square miles by the granting of provincial status to Manitoba in 1870 and Alberta and Saskatchewan in 1905, and as an indirect result of the Yukon Gold Rush of 1896. When gold lured thousands of prospectors, many of them Americans, to the sparsely populated Yukon, the Canadian government, fearing an American takeover, formally brought the Yukon Territory into being in 1898. Today the Northwest Territories, lying west of Hudson Bay, north of latitude 60°, and east of the Yukon Territory, occupy more than one-third of Canada's land area: a vast region of craggy mountains, countless lakes, windswept tundra, wild rivers, brilliant northern lights and mosquito-plagued bogs.

Geologists find the territories fascinating. Here are

three distinct mountain areas: the Mackenzie Mountains (the border with the Yukon); the mountains of southern Baffin Island (a part of the ancient Appalachian system); and the towering ranges of north Baffin Island, Ellesmere Island and the other islands of the Arctic Archipelago. "Forbidding" is the only way to describe Ellesmere Island's immense peaks; to this day they remain beyond the reach of the most daring mountaineers.

The territories' most prized geological feature is the Canadian (Precambrian) Shield. Seen from the air – the best way to try to grasp the size and diversity of the Northwest Territories – the shield appears as a crazy jumble of rocks girding Hudson Bay like a battered horseshoe. Little wonder they look so well-worn, for the shield was formed more than 600 million years ago, and its rocks are the geological heart of North America.

West and north of the shield lie great plains, cousins of the prairies to the south. Like the prairies, these northern plains are the remnants of long vanished inland seas and lakes. Created from the sediments left behind by these extinct waters, their strata is rich in oil and natural gas.

Dog teams and sledges these pages, for centuries the only means of crossing vast wastelands of snow and ice, are now being superseded by snowmobiles, tractors and helicopters. The ice-blue eyes of the dogs traditionally associated with trans-Arctic travel seem to reflect the very color of their inhospitable environment. Nowadays, dog-sleigh racing above is becoming an increasingly popular sport, demanding both courage and stamina.

The mighty Mackenzie River, whose enormous 700,000-square-mile basin could comfortably accommodate Great Britain eight times over, rises high in the B.C. Rockies. Before it departs on its true journey from Great Slave Lake, it has already received the waters of the Parsnip, Peace, Athabaska, and Slave Rivers – some of North America's largest river systems. Now, on its thousand-mile journey to the arctic waters of the Beaufort Sea, the Mackenzie continues to be fed by countless tributaries, the largest of which is B.C.'s Liard River. When the rough and tumble Liard meets the Mackenzie near Fort Simpson, the tale of the Liard's hard journey through sandstone gorges and rocky mountains is easily read in the churning sediments it disgorges into the pristine Mackenzie. Of all the Liard's many tributaries, nothing quite rivals the wild, tempestuous Nahanni, whose boiling, foam-crested rapids are an unrivalled challenge for those with nerve enough to raft these racing white waters.

When the snow and ice of the long northern winter close in, it is hard to distinguish land from river. Even Great Bear Lake, an immense inland sea bested in size only by three of the Great Lakes – Superior, Huron, and Michigan – is usually frozen until the last week in July. To dip one's hand into Great Bear Lake is to experience such paralyzing cold that it seems impossible that one's blood will ever flow again.

Any map of the territories shows the labyrinth of rivers, lakes, and streams that ebb and flow through this huge region. Maps also show that the Northwest Territories appear to be cut in half at 66° 33 minutes north latitude – the delineation of the Arctic Circle. If you live in the Arctic Circle, you can expect little or no sight of the sun for at least three months during winter, while summer will bring three months or more of continuous daylight.

The long night that is a northern winter is, however, illuminated not only by the moon and the stars – and the heavens here are wondrously clear and sharp – but also by the brilliance of the *aurora borealis*, those multi-hued dancing streamers of light caused by the interaction of charged particles from the sun and the Earth's magnetic poles.

In addition to the Arctic Circle, another line splits the territories. The treeline, which winds haphazardly southeast from the Mackenzie Delta on the Beaufort Sea to the northeast tip of Manitoba on Hudson Bay, divides the Northwest Territories into two distinct geographic areas, taiga and tundra. South of the treeline is the taiga, a land of scrub, intermittent stands of spruce, larch and white birch.

The endless arctic tundra occupies the region north of the treeline. This land is known as the Barrens, or more picturesquely, as the Land of Little Sticks. With mean July temperatures of less than 10°C., no trees can survive here.

THE YUKON & THE NORTHWEST TERRITORIES

The rock-strewn tundra can only nourish grass-like plants, mosses and lichens, which provide grazing for herds of musk oxen and caribou. The blessed warmth of summer is heralded annually by the bright pinks and yellows of the host of tiny, land-hugging arctic flowers that also grow on the tundra.

In both taiga and tundra, summer frees the land from the freezing grip of permafrost. A distinctly northern phenomenon, permafrost, or permanently frozen ground, is a rock-hard mixture of soil, stone and ice. In summer when the surface permafrost thaws, a few inches of spongy soil or a deep mushy bog result. Whatever

Frobisher Bay above and facing page *has been designated the center for education, administration and economic development for the eastern Arctic. It has its own airport, which serves as the* starting point for many tourists interested in exploring this extraordinary region. From Frobisher Bay, it is only one stop to Resolute, a stone's throw from the magnetic North Pole.

happens on the surface, the ground core remains frozen solid preventing any deep plant roots from taking hold and denying a subsurface drainage system for water. Permafrost makes the land of the Northwest Territories quick to sustain injury and incredibly slow to heal. One of the most fascinating byproducts of permafrost are pingos, giant boils, with a solid core of ice, that erupt from the earth and gradually become covered with soil and vegetation. Pingos on the Mackenzie Delta flats can be as high as 240 feet.

As the warmth of the sun melts the ice on the territories' rivers and lakes, it opens the lid on a veritable Pandora's box of whirring, biting insects. Blackflies, bulldog flies, and mosquitoes are ferocious in these parts, swarming relentlessly around man and beast alike. Animals are driven insane by these devouring tyrants and a day-spent in a cloud of continuously humming – and biting – mosquitoes is enough to unstring the hardiest human.

Despite its seemingly desolate appearance, the Northwest Territories have a varied ecosystem. Some seventy-five different species of birds, including the rare peregrine falcon, migrate here each summer to breed, joining those hardier year-round residents, the feather-footed ptarmigans, owls, jet black ravens, and assorted gulls. Of all the summer residents, the tern has the farthest to travel. Each year these hardy birds fly in from the

Antarctic, breed, and return home at the end of summer, a round trip flight of almost 14,000 miles.

Enormous walleye, arctic grayling and northern pike pack the territories' rivers, streams and lakes. Great sea mammals – beluga whales, white whales, narwhals, walruses, and seals – thrive on the rich marine vegetation of the Arctic Ocean. Polar bears are kings of the sea ice, and caribou graze the tundra in their multitudes. There are at least seven major caribou herds in the Northwest Territories, and the sight of one of these great herds, generally about 100,000 strong, on the move to summer pastures is truly awesome. Equally awe-inspiring are the herds of musk oxen, the bulls formed in a protective circle around the cows and calves, their great shaggy coats ruffled by the winds that blow over the high arctic islands where they prefer to graze. The Mackenzie Valley is moose territory, while grizzlies and black bears rule the mountains of the west. Great white wolves and the beautiful arctic fox, large white hares and the prolific little mouse-like lemming are all Northwest Territories natives.

Likewise indigenous to the territories, at least by virtue of their long residency there, are the majority of its 45,000 citizens, some 29,000 of whom are descendants of Asian peoples who first started to cross the present-day Bering Strait by a vast land bridge some 25,000 years ago. These migrations are believed to have continued up to about 5,000 years ago.

The first arrivals were the ancestors of today's Dene people, who currently number about 8,500. The Inuit, often erroneously called "Eskimos," were apparently the last to migrate to the north. Today there are about 16,000 descendants of those long ago immigrants from Siberia, living for the most part in the tundra region, as their forebears did. The taiga continues to be the traditional home of the Dene. The Métis, some 4,500 in number, look to both the native peoples and the early European explorers and fur traders for their ancestry.

European interest in the north was orginally restricted to its waters. Sebastian Cabot sailed to the north in 1508, looking for a northwest passage route to the Orient. In 1576, England's Sir Martin Frobisher, likewise pursuing Cabot's dream, landed on Baffin Island where he mistakenly took iron pyrites, "fool's gold," for the real thing, causing a minor gold rush.

Although this gold rush was a fiasco, while it lasted it was responsible for bringing intrepid navigators to the uncharted northern waters. Men like Henry Hudson, who in 1610 sailed into the great bay that bears his name, did much to fill in the empty spaces on the maps and charts of the north.

In the end furs, not gold, established the European presence in the north. The Hudson's Bay Company, founded in 1670, built forts at the mouths of the rivers emptying into Hudson Bay, and encouraged the Dene to bring the glossy beaver and fox pelts to the forts for trade. At the same time, the company's trader-explorers set out to chart the coast and the northern sealanes. In 1771, Samuel Hearne, looking for copper, discovered the Coppermine River and became the first white man to see the inner reaches of the polar sea. Eighteen years later, Alexander Mackenzie of the rival North West Company, journeyed the route of his namesake river. While on his famous voyage, Mackenzie noticed oil seepages on the river banks. Oil being of little use in the eighteenth

century, Mackenzie's find created almost no interest.

The region became the talk of Europe after Captain John Franklin disappeared there while on a voyage of exploration in 1845. Efforts to discover the fate of Franklin's expedition yielded much geographic data about the north, but no word of Franklin and his 129 men. Finally, in 1859, a cairn was found on King William Island in which were preserved records of Franklin's death in 1847 and of the sad fate of the crew. With their leader dead and their ships stuck fast in the polar ice, Franklin's men had set off over the frozen wastes of the Boothia Peninsula to journey to the south. There were no survivors.

Today, the oil that Mackenzie paid such little attention to almost two centuries ago holds the key to much of Canada's hopes for energy self-sufficiency. Commercial oil development first got under way around 1921 at Norman Wells, on the Mackenzie River, just west of Great Bear Lake. Now there are vast offshore drilling efforts going on in the Beaufort Sea and on the various arctic islands.

Exploration and drilling under such adverse conditions are horrendously expensive, as, indeed, is transporting the oil to southern markets. But deposits of both oil – estimated at about 36 billion barrels – and natural gas – said to occupy 339 trillion cubic feet – are high enough to warrant the enormous extraction and delivery costs.

Drilling in the high arctic is a test of engineering ingenuity. Faced with winter ice often more than six feet thick and the constant jostles of moving pack ice and floating ice islands, engineers propose anchoring their derricks on artificial islands. These landfast ice zones, designed not only for exploratory drilling but also for full-scale production, are formed with great quantities of sand dredged from the ocean floor.

Besides the cost of such ventures, both drilling and the transportation of hydro-carbons pose a threat to the territories' fragile ecosystem. Oil blow-ups, ruptured pipelines, and tanker spills spell sure disaster to the marine and land creatures of the north. The concern of the Dene and Inuit over this possible irreparable damage to the north led to the postponement of the Mackenzie Valley gas pipeline and to a much closer look at the impact of mineral development on the north.

In addition to oil and gas, the territories are one of the world's great treasure troves of non-renewable resources. Mining is the backbone of the territories' economy. Gold, silver, copper, lead tungsten, zinc, cadmium, bismuth, coal and asbestos are the principal minerals mined.

At present, the Northwest Territories are under the same forms of administration as the Yukon. Administering government and social services in such a vast area poses an enormous organizational problem. To overcome this, the territories are divided into four administrative regions, each with its own regional headquarters: Inuvik, Fort Smith, Keewatin, and Baffin Island.

Pictured left is Whitehorse, the capital of the Yukon Territory. Founded during the Klondike Gold Rush in 1897-8, Whitehorse has been a capital since 1952. It is the Yukon headquarters of the Royal Canadian Mounted Police, and an important transportation center on the Alaska Highway.
Overleaf A winter landscape.

Despite the rapid advance of modern technology, the old ways linger. Dogs work as a team pulling a sled along a *track lined with telegraph poles above, while facing page an Inuit woman wears traditional fur clothing.*

Unlike the Yukon, where, outside of Whitehorse, communities are very few and sparsely populated, the Northwest Territories have five centers with populations topping 2,000: Yellowknife, Inuvik, Frobisher Bay, Fort Smith, and Hay River.

Set on a rocky peninsula of Great Slave Lake, Yellowknife, the territories' capital, is a city of 6,000 people. In the 1930s, it was a tent city serving the needs of miners who had come to work in the nearby gold fields. Half a century later, it is still a mining town, but now it is a splendidly located modern community of tall apartment buildings and shopping centers. Its population seems to be always on the move, with Inuit, Dene and Métis coming and going from all over the territories, and people from southern Canada doing likewise at the start or finish of northern postings.

Some 325 miles south of the Arctic Circle, Yellowknife is accessible from Alberta by the Mackenzie Highway. There is no bridge at the Mackenzie River

THE YUKON & THE NORTHWEST TERRITORIES

the Mackenzie Highway arrived here in 1949.

West of Hay River is Fort Simpson, on the junction of the Mackenzie and Liard rivers. Not surprisingly, this town, too, started off as a fur trading post, which it still is, making Fort Simpson the oldest such post in continuous use. Fort Simpson is also a good source of supplies for wilderness explorers off to confront Nahanni National Park.

Situated in the southwest corner of the territories, remote Nahanni follows the course of the savage, unpredictable South Nahanni River. The park is an unspoiled delight of abundant wildlife and distinct vegetation. Here are the ancient Rabbitkettle Hot Springs and the mighty Virginia Falls, which are almost twice the height of Ontario's Niagara Falls.

Thanks to the Dempster Highway, intrepid motorists can set off from Whitehorse in the Yukon, cross the Arctic Circle and proceed to Inuvik on the Mackenzie Delta. Be prepared for 750 miles of rough gravel roads. But the scenery is glorious, the wildlife plentiful but shy, and you will be travelling the route followed by Inspector William Dempster of the North West Mounted Police in his quest for a missing patrol of Mounties. Dempster found his men, but not before they had perished in the cold, so take note.

Inuvik is the major commercial, transportation and communications center for the Mackenzie Delta and the main supply base for petro-chemical exploration in the area. Inuvik was built in 1955 to replace Aklavik, situated opposite it across the Mackenzie River in the Yukon, which had been devastated by serious flooding. But Aklavik refused to die, so today Aklavik and Inuvik are twin communities.

To the north is Tuktoyaktuk, or Tuk, as the locals call it. (The name means "looks like a caribou." Situated on the shores of the Beaufort Sea, 100 miles south of the Arctic Ocean's permanent polar ice cap, Tuk is famous for its pingos, and for the beautiful muskrat, seal and wolfskin parkas fashioned by the Inuit women of the town's Nuak cooperative.

Tuk became a permanent settlement in 1934 when the Hudson's Bay Company transferred its post from Herchel Island to the town. The traditional pursuits of trapping, whaling, sealing and reindeer herding continue, but are fast being eclipsed by oil exploration. Offshore drilling pays the rent for most Tuk citizens. The town is also a transportation base for high arctic communities.

North of the Amundsen Gulf are the islands of the Arctic Archipelago: Banks, Victoria, Melville, Prince of Wales, Somerset, King William, and Parry. Frobisher Bay, the largest community in the district, is situated on southern Baffin Island. Just forty years old, Frobisher grew up around a United States airforce landing strip, becoming in the 1950s the logistics base for the DEW line. Frobisher today bustles with government and private enterprises, among which are several outlets for Inuit art and handicrafts – parkas, knitwear, gold and silver jewelry.

Although Inukitut, the main Inuit language, has no word for art, it does contain a word meaning "to make something the very best you can." Certainly the Inuit's arts and crafts – as well as their very way of life – are fashioned with this thought in mind.

Ironically, while few Canadians ever see the true north, its vastness is an essential part of the Canadian identity as inhabitants of a free, untramelled land.

crossing, however, and the ferry only runs during the summer. At other times you must fly.

Most northerners fly everywhere. Indeed, without aircraft most of the north would not be reachable at all. Aircraft first came to the territories to serve the Norman Wells oil fields. Today, Canadian airlines maintain daily services to the major northern centers, bringing in everything from powdered milk to circuit judges. Back in the 1920s, northern skies were the preserve of a gallant bunch of ex-World War I fighter pilots – men like "Wop" May and "Punch" Dickens – who flew their tiny planes all over the arctic. A leading Canadian historian once remarked that "the whole history of the Canadian north can be divided into two parts – before and after the airplane." Certainly without the pioneer efforts of the first bush pilots, the communities of the north would never have come into being. Yellowknife's fine monument to their endeavors records their pride of place in the north.

Across Great Slave Lake on the southern shore is Hay River, a busy port town of 3,500 people. Here barges bound for far-flung arctic settlements load up with everything from candy bars to whole houses. Though the town began as a fur post in 1868, it really only came into its own when

First published in Canada 1982 by
Collins Publishers, 100 Lesmill Road, Don Mills, Ontario.
© 1982 Text: Collins Publishers
© 1982 Illustrations: Colour Library International Ltd.,
    New Malden, Surrey, England.
Color separations by FERCROM, Barcelona, Spain.
Display and text filmsetting by ACESETTERS LTD.,
    Richmond, Surrey, England.
Printed and bound in Barcelona, Spain by JISA-RIEUSSET
    & EUROBINDER.

Canadian Cataloging in Publication Data.

Deutsch, Grace, 1947-
    Canada, a symphony in color.

ISBN 0-00-216865-0 – UK ISBN 0-00-218013-8

1. Canada – Description and travel – 1950-   – Views.*
I. Swan, Avanthia. II. Title.

FC75.D49   917.1'04646'0222   C82-094214-6
F1016.D49

The publisher would like to thank the Canadian High
Commission, Tourism Section, for the loan of
transparencies of Prince Edward Island.

**The publishers acknowledge with thanks the assistance
provided by AIR CANADA in the production of this book.**